Rage

True Stories By Teens About Anger

Edited By Laura Longhine Of Youth Communication

EasyRead Large

Copyright Page from the Original Book

Copyright © 2012 by Youth Communication

All rights reserved under International and Pan-American Copyright Conventions. Unless otherwise noted, no part of this book may be reproduced, stored in a retrieval system, or transmitted in any form or by any means, electronic, mechanical, photocopying, recording, or otherwise, without express written permission of the publisher, except for brief quotations or critical reviews. For more information, go to www.freespirit.com/company/permissions.cfm.

Free Spirit, Free Spirit Publishing, and associated logos are trademarks and/or registered trademarks of Free Spirit Publishing Inc. A complete listing of our logos and trademarks is available at www.freespirit.com.

Library of Congress Cataloging-in-Publication Data
Longhine, Laura.
    Rage : true stories by teens about anger / edited by Laura Longhine.
        p. cm. — (Real teen voices series)
    Includes index.
    ISBN 978-1-57542-414-9 — ISBN 1-57542-414-2 1. Anger in adolescence—Juvenile literature. I. Title.
    BF724.3.A55.L66 2012
    155.5'1247—dc23
                                                                                                                  2012016889

eBook ISBN: 978-1-57542-656-3

> Free Spirit Publishing does not have control over or assume responsibility for author or third-party websites and their content. At the time of this book's publication, all facts and figures cited within are the most current available. All telephone numbers, addresses, and website URLs are accurate and active as of May 2012. If you find an error or believe that a resource listed here is not as described, please contact Free Spirit Publishing. Parents, teachers, and other adults: We strongly urge you to monitor children's use of the Internet.

Reading Level Grades 9 & up; Interest Level Ages 13 & up;
Fountas & Pinnell Guided Reading Level Z+

Photo credits from Dreamstime.com: cover © Ljupco, p. 5 © Dnf-style, p. 15 © Pcheruvi, p. 26 © Geotrac, p. 34 © Velkol, p. 45 © Ronfromyork, p. 56 © Epantha, p. 67 © Vlue, p. 78 © Nickp37, p. 87 © Braendan, p. 96 © Msymons, p. 103 © Imagesolution, p. 110 © Xaoc, p. 119 © Marianmocanu, p. 127 © Fotosmile, p. 135 © Cwd, p. 140 © Caravana, p. 151 © Lostbear, p. 155 © Edoma

Cover and interior design by Tasha Kenyon

10 9 8 7 6 5 4 3 2
Printed in the United States of America
S18860513

Free Spirit Publishing Inc.
Minneapolis, MN
(612) 338-2068
help4kids@freespirit.com
www.freespirit.com

Free Spirit offers competitive pricing.
Contact edsales@freespirit.com for pricing information on
multiple quantity purchases.

TABLE OF CONTENTS

INTRODUCTION	ii
THE FURY DEEP INSIDE	1
LOOSE CANNON	15
KARATE KILLED THE MONSTER INSIDE ME	30
BUM-RUSHED BY THE PAST	41
THE MONSTER INSIDE	57
FINDING FREEDOM	73
INVISIBLE MAN	87
WRESTLING WITH MY ANGER	102
ESCAPING THE PRISON OF ANGER	115
EXPLAINING MY LIFE	129
TAMING MY ANGER	139
THE LIFE AND DEATH OF THE CRIPPLED ENIGMA	148
READY TO FIGHT	162
RELEASING MY RAGE	173
TEMPER TAMERS?	184
CHANGING THE PATTERN	191
ANGER THAT WON'T LET GO	207
HOW TO CHILL OUT	214
ABOUT YOUTH COMMUNICATION	221
ABOUT THE EDITOR	223
Real Teen Voices Series	224
BACK COVER MATERIAL	228
Index	231

"Teens will identify with the writers, discover that their own problems are not unique, and be encouraged to find help, making these titles solid choices."

—*School Library Journal*

INTRODUCTION

The teen years can be tumultuous—a time of flux and personal discovery. Classes get tougher, demands and expectations get higher, relationships with friends and family are changing—even bodies are changing. But some teens also deal with losing contact with family members, being bullied, growing up with abuse or neglect, or having to live with strangers who don't care for them. Some teens are in situations where they are not able to express their feelings, or they learn to express their feelings in destructive ways.

As a result, teens may have a hard time knowing what they feel. As many of the teen writers in this book explain, anger becomes the only emotion they have left. And though expressing their rage can feel empowering in the moment, uncontrollable anger usually leaves teens feeling powerless. It can lead to serious consequences and threaten their goals for the future.

In these essays, teens write about their struggles with anger and describe how their abusive pasts have affected their emotions. They are frank about the negative ways they've let out their feelings, but also write about learning to express themselves in more positive ways.

Many of the writers talk about an anger that feels out of control, but which they desperately want to contain.

In "The Monster Inside," Griffin K. writes about his struggle to stop himself from releasing his rage on the people around him: "When I look back, I see that I was always waiting for someone to intervene, someone to stop me—the teachers, my counselor, security, or the police. When I was hurting someone, I was looking around like a child, hoping someone would take control of the monster inside me."

The writers are honest about the fact that controlling their anger is often an ongoing struggle. But they also show that it's possible to get help, both from other people and on their own.

The teens in this book have learned many strategies for keeping calm, including deep breathing, counting, knitting, drawing, cleaning, listening to music, dancing, playing sports, spending time with friends, reading self-help books, walking away from arguments, and trying to avoid upsetting situations. Most importantly, the teens find that learning to express their emotions, and not bottling up their pain, helps them control their anger.

Good therapists help several writers open up about their feelings. When Fred W. talks in an anger management group, he feels relieved. "Letting out some of my emotions was the best thing I've done," he writes. "It helped me find out who I was. It felt great to break my family's taboo against talking about our feelings or discussing what happened inside our house."

A sympathetic new foster parent helps Julie Stewart start to express herself. "By opening up her heart and home to me, she gave me a feeling of belonging," Julie says about her new foster mom. "She talked with me about the emotions I had from all the abuse, and that in itself made me feel a little less angry."

And Otis Hampton finds that writing is a way to let out his emotions: "I'd like to keep my anger on the page and out of my life as much as I can."

Regardless of the strategies they use, learning how to deal with painful emotions in a safe way lets teens regain a sense of safety and control.

The stories in this book offer a window into many teens' lives. You are sure to find within its pages people and experiences you can identify with and relate to. You might find that you can get more out of the book by applying what the writers have learned to your own life. The teens who wrote these stories did so because they hope that telling their stories will help readers who are facing similar challenges. They want you to know that you are not alone, and that taking specific steps can help you manage or overcome very difficult situations. They've done their best to be clear about the actions that worked for them so you can see if they'll work for you. For further help, this book also features interviews with therapists and psychologists about the causes of anger, how it affects people, how to identify what triggers it, and how to handle anger in healthy ways.

Another way to use the book is to develop your writing skills. Each teen in this book wrote 5 to 10 drafts of his or her story before it was published. If you read the stories closely you'll see that the teens work to include a beginning, a middle, and an end, along with good scenes, description, dialogue, and anecdotes (little stories). To improve your writing, take a look at how these writers construct their stories. Try some of their techniques in your own writing.

If you'd like more information about the writing program at Youth Communication or want to read more teen essays, visit www.youthcomm.org.

THE FURY DEEP INSIDE

by Julie Stewart

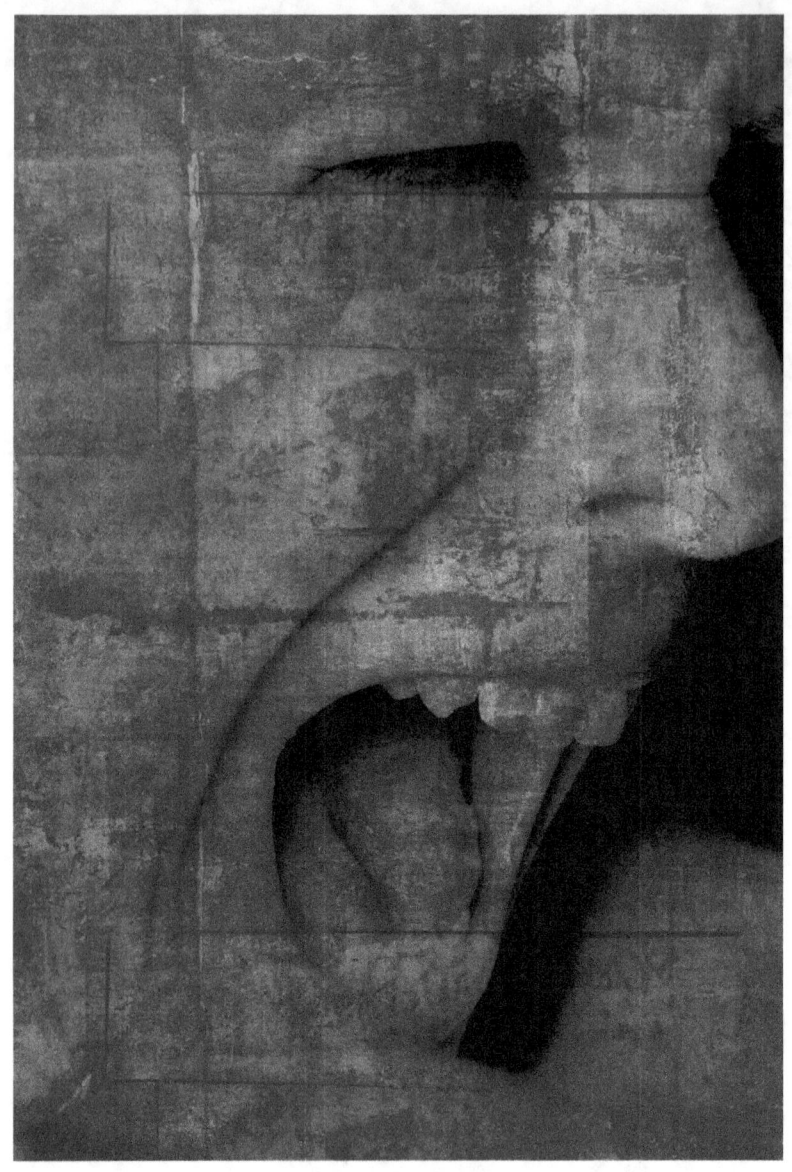

For half of my life, "abuse me" seemed to be my middle name. I was abused in all the ways you could imagine, and this had a big impact on me. It took hold of my emotions. It stripped me of my innocence until I felt like there was no hope left. The anger of those who abused me bounced off of them and onto me. This was something I had to deal with on my own. I had to learn how to manage the anger I carried around.

> **The anger of those who abused me bounced off of them and onto me.**

When I was 7 I was placed in my first foster home with a lady I'll call Ms. L. By then, I had already experienced abuse. Still, I was usually a mellow kind of person. I never had an attitude problem unless someone was cruel to me. When people were cruel to me, I sometimes threatened them, but usually I just kept quiet.

When I moved to Ms. L's house, my anger grew and grew. It grew until I thought I would explode with it. I couldn't keep quiet anymore.

At first, Ms. L seemed like a sweet old lady. She and I had a mother-daughter relationship. She said a lot of "I love yous" and gave a lot of hugs and kisses, something that I always wanted my biological mother to do for me. Getting this love felt good.

Days turned into months and her ways started to change. After about two years of living with her, she started becoming violent toward me. I'm not sure why she changed, maybe because I was getting older and was no longer a little girl. Whatever the reason, I lived with this violence for seven years.

The abuse first started when she said something harsh about my mother. She said, "Your mother is a crackhead who will never amount to anything and will never get you home because she never wanted you in the first place. That's why she hates you."

These words affected me profoundly. They hurt, and I felt there was more hurt to come. I was right.

One day I was playing in the backyard and I slipped on the plants.

Ms. L saw me slip. She thought I was playing in the garden so she ran outside and rushed like somebody was out to get her. She slapped me hard across my face. I was thinking, "If she really loves me, why did she hurt me?"

After that, the abuse went on almost every day. Sometimes she would hit me with whatever was lying around. If her slippers were lying around, she'd hit me with them.

My anger started around this time. I began exploding at my friends and loved ones. If someone close to me took their bad day out on me, I would get really frustrated and start saying harsh things to hurt them. Then I would turn around and regret everything I said. My emotions felt out of control.

My anger came from the abuse I had experienced throughout my life, and from the silence I didn't break when I had had enough of it. Nobody seemed to care two egg rolls about me. It made me so angry. I wanted to walk away from those feelings so much.

But I couldn't walk away from my anger and I couldn't control my temper. Soon I wasn't just getting angry at people who disrespected me first. I'd start fights in school with my best friends. I used profanity against teachers who were trying to help me. I hurt my own family with harsh words. This attitude of mine was careless. I didn't want anybody to befriend me. I was too scary and angry to love, I thought, so I made a point of hurting them before they hurt me.

> **I didn't want anybody to befriend me. I was too scary and angry to love, I thought, so I made a point of hurting them before they hurt me.**

I knew I had a serious anger problem when I started to beat on my baby sister, who was about 5. I struck her hard across the face when she said a word to me that I myself had taught her, the word "b—." Then I felt bad. I knew I was doing what adults had always done to me—I was taking my problems out on someone smaller, someone who didn't deserve it one bit.

But Ms. L kept abusing me and I kept silent about it. I still needed a way to vent my anger. Sometimes I just tried to escape my problems. I took walks and daydreamed to make the pain go away.

Taking long walks in the park after school made my thoughts simmer down, and I was always relieved not to be going straight home to Ms. L. But whenever I walked I could almost hear the clock ticking, and I worried that Ms. L would soon be out searching for me, for the rule was to come straight home after school.

One day I felt especially rebellious. I took a really long walk. Seconds turned into minutes and the speed of my steps quickened. I didn't want to go back. Not yet. I wanted more moments of peace.

Then something caught my attention. A car I recognized pulled onto the sidewalk. Ms. L jumped out of it and grabbed my arm. I could have known who it was just by her grip. She screamed at me and punched me in front of a bunch of people. When we got home, the day went on like any other, her hitting me again and again.

I knew I couldn't take it anymore. The abuse and the rage took over my heart. One day in the middle of fall, my friend Latoya started talking about how she wanted to leave her adoptive family because of the way they treated her, so I suggested that we run away together.

That's just what we did, like Thelma and Louise. We went first to my grandmother's house, who let us stay for one night only. The next day my uncle let us stay in his apartment. He said that he would have to call my caseworker. Latoya went home.

The next morning as the hours went by, I waited impatiently for my caseworker to pick me up. I was looking forward to it, because I had decided I would tell my caseworker about the abuse. Then I would never have to go back to Ms. L's house again.

When the caseworker finally arrived, we sat and talked. I let everything out this time. It felt scary but good to let all the pain be released from my heart through talking. The caseworker thought I should have told somebody earlier about the abuse, and she was angry at

Ms. L. She said that her rights as a foster parent would be taken away. Then she thanked me for being courageous and telling her.

> **It felt scary but good to let all the pain be released from my heart through talking.**

It turns out that running away had a big impact on my life. It made the anger that I had simmer down a little because I knew I wouldn't be going back to Ms. L's house. It also made me feel like I had more control over my environment. I had gotten myself out of a bad situation. That made me feel like I had more control.

I then was placed in a home with a loving family and a lady named Lucille Hardison. It was hard at first. I didn't know what to expect from the family. But soon I realized that their home felt different from Ms. L's.

Ms. Hardison sometimes talked about the problems in my life like I was part of the family. She told me straight up that she felt the abuse that I had faced in Ms. L's home wasn't right. She explained that she didn't believe in hitting kids. She said that you must work with children, not hit them.

Her telling me that made me feel like there were decent people in the world. And that helped me open up to her and trust her. I felt like I was no longer alone with my problems.

Ms. Hardison grew to be like a grandmother to me. By opening up her heart and home to me, she gave me a feeling of belonging. When it came to my anger problem, she worked with me step by step and never gave up on me. She talked with me about the emotions I had from all the abuse, and that in itself made me feel a little less angry.

I also started to realize that my temper had a good side to it: it had brought me back to life. It had opened up my eyes and shown me that I couldn't keep living with all the abuse I had put up with for so long. It had given me the courage to get out of a bad situation.

Still, I no longer wanted that anger to be controlling me. Sometimes, even with Ms. Hardison's help, trying to control that evil force in my heart felt hopeless. So I prayed to God to help me. That gave me strength to go forward even when the world felt its darkest.

It also helped to talk to some of my family members about my problem. They encouraged me and told me that whenever I needed them they would be there no matter what. It felt good to know my family would stick by my side even through bad times.

I especially had trouble controlling my temper around my mother. Whenever she acted selfishly toward me, I felt hatred all over. I thought of the times I had experienced abuse living with her, and wished that I had spoken to someone about it back then.

> **Once I started learning to control my anger, I realized I didn't know who I was without it. That was scary. It left me feeling confused and a little helpless for a while.**

But I also realized that having experienced all that made me even more determined not to hit kids for no reason. That gave me more motivation to work on my temper, and, slowly, I taught myself how to relax my mind and not snap over something that wasn't worth it. Instead, I found that crying, speaking about my anger, taking a walk, or cleaning helped me feel better.

I discovered that there was a strange consequence to me learning to control my temper. For so many years, I'd lived with so much anger that I'd started to think that that was all there was to me. Once I started learning to control my anger, I realized I didn't know who I was without it. That was scary. I didn't know how to act if I didn't act with anger. It left me feeling confused and a little helpless for a while.

Over time, though, I began to feel more comfortable not living with so much anger. I'm not saying that I don't have any temper now. I still do. When I get mad, my emotions sometimes still take over, especially when I'm angry because a family member or my boyfriend has disappointed me. But now instead of lashing out at others because of my hurt, I'll do something else to clear my mind.

I especially like cleaning. You know how when you're cleaning and you want to get things right? It feels like everything is connected: I can get a room together and my thoughts together at the same time. Every time I pick up something to put it away, I pretend I'm picking up my problems and throwing them away or putting them in their place. While I do that, I listen to mellow music to soothe my mood. By the time I see the person I'm mad at, my attitude toward them has changed. I can talk to them about what bothers me more calmly.

Last Christmas, I wanted a specific pair of black boots. I'd wanted those boots forever. I thought I was definitely going to get them from my mother. When my mother said that I wouldn't receive the boots, I felt very hurt and mad. I felt myself losing my temper.

My mother explained that she didn't have the money to get me the boots and that she was sorry. Normally, I wouldn't have listened. I would have made her feel bad and wouldn't try to understand her point of view because it was all about me, me, me.

But this time, I calmed myself down. I tried to really listen to her, and eventually I felt in my heart that she was really sorry, which made me feel better. It also felt like I was growing up. It made me feel in control of my life and emotions.

Over time, I have been getting to know myself more. I am seeing that there is a lot more to me than my anger.

LOOSE CANNON

by Fred W.

"How do you plead to the assault, Frederick?" I looked up at the judge who held my life in his hands.

"Guilty," I squeaked, tears falling down my face.

The judge told me that because I'd told the truth and pleaded guilty, he was giving me a shorter sentence. (I learned the hard way that if I didn't get with the program, my short sentence would grow and grow.) He sent me to Sagamore, a lockdown facility, until the state could find me a residential program with anger management classes.

"Your Honor, can I give my son one last hug before he goes?" asked my mother.

"Permission granted."

She gave me a hug and then I was taken out of the courtroom into the unknown.

Rage had led me to that courtroom. It started when I was 4 years old and my father started sniffing cocaine. His cocaine use and my parents' drinking led them to fights that became an all-out war.

Here's a typical fight: My good-for-nothing father calls my mother a whore because some guy in the bowling alley told my mother, "You look good! Why are you with a deadbeat?"

At home, my brother and I sit on the couch while all hell breaks loose. My parents look like the old Tom and Jerry cartoons when Spike would beat up Jerry in a tornado of fists, legs, and screams.

Once, my mom pulled a knife from the kitchen. I covered my brother's eyes and watched in horror as my father egged on my mother. She stabbed my father's chest four times, though not deeply. It was so horrible that I passed out.

> **It was terrifying to experience my parents' violence. The damage they inflicted on each other made me fear them both. My fear turned into a rage that consumed me and burned all who tried to reach out to me.**

It was terrifying to experience my parents' violence. The damage they inflicted on each other made me fear them both. Then my father started to abuse me physically and sexually. My fear turned into a rage that consumed me and burned all who tried to reach out to me.

At 13, I was quiet and shy. I pretty much kept to myself. But because of what my father did to me, when I got angry I went straight into a rage.

That year, someone spread a rumor in school that I was going to shoot a kid named Zeko with a shotgun. I don't know why the rumor spread—hate, jealousy, whatever. Zeko believed it, which I thought was funny.

One day I was coming out of school with some friends. We were slap boxing when Zeko walked by and said, "Take Fred's head off!" I believed Zeko was out to get me. "Crap, Zeko is plotting something and it's my funeral!" I thought.

As I was walking home—fast—Zeko popped out of a large crowd and swung at my face. CRACK! He knocked my tooth in and flung me against the fence. I got up and pulled out the knife I often carried. Soon I gave up my chase and went home, holding my tooth in agony and defeat.

For the next few weeks, I lived in constant fear. I was afraid my attacker lurked around every corner, waiting to strike again.

A few weeks later, we had a school dance. I was having a great time with my friends until I saw Zeko on the other side of the gym, grilling me with what looked like seething hate. I grilled him back and flipped him off to see if he was gonna pop off.

He walked over and flinched at me. I was scared but thought, "There are mad females here. I can't look like a punk. Plus, I don't want to be hit again." Using my messed up logic, I hit him.

I just meant to shock him, but once I hit him, I blacked out. I didn't feel or see anything until a friend pulled me off. Looking at Zeko, I saw his bloody, lumpy, and bruised face.

My friends told me, "Get out of here before security gets into the gym." Three friends took me home. I was confused and mad. "Why the hell did you help me with the fight? I could have handled Zeko myself!" I yelled.

"Fred, you did that yourself," one friend told me.

"Really?" I asked, surprised and impressed with myself. "Boy, revenge is sweet!"

After that night, I pushed the fight out of my head. I still couldn't remember hitting Zeko, and I didn't know he was seriously injured. But a few months later, the police came to my school and arrested me.

I thought I'd be let go. It was just a fight. The severity didn't hit me until I got charged with assault and locked up. My mom dropped off my clothes at the facility I would call home for three months while I waited for my trial. After that, she visited me only a few times—just enough to keep the courts off her back. (Once they learned about my home life, they were threatening to charge my mom with neglect.)

For the first two weeks, I cried myself to sleep. Even though my family life wasn't good, I missed them and couldn't comprehend living apart from my family for so long. I felt very alone.

After the trial, I got sent to Sagamore and was placed in the male mental ward. I was enraged, thinking, "Why am I here? Please, someone help!" Eventually someone did help, but it wasn't the help I wanted.

> **In my family there was an unspoken contract not to talk about feelings, probably because our anger and sadness would have been too much to deal with.**

That summer, I got transferred to St. Mary's, an all-male residential treatment center on Long Island, outside of New York City. I went to school, took anger management classes, ate, and slept. Anger management classes really sucked. The staff tried to get us to talk about our feelings, but in my family there was an unspoken contract not to talk about feelings, probably because our anger and sadness would have been too much to deal with.

I thought the questions the staff asked about my crime were corny.

"Fred, why did you hit the kid?"

"I was happy, what the hell do you think?" I said. Never again did I talk in that group.

I saw myself as a struggling young man trying to handle my life. The facility saw me as a danger to the community because I was a loose cannon. Since I wouldn't deal with my feelings in the group, the staff figured that I'd beat the crap out of anybody who said something wrong to me.

> **The facility saw me as a danger to the community because I was a loose cannon. Since I wouldn't deal with my feelings in the group, the staff figured that I'd beat the crap out of anybody who said something wrong to me.**

I was only supposed to be at St. Mary's for one year. But because I wouldn't participate, the judge kept extending my placement, from one year to two, then three, then four. My fourth year at St. Mary's was rough. The staff kept telling me that if I didn't talk, the judge would send me upstate to a tougher facility. That came true. At 17,

I got sent to Goshen Residential Center, a sugarcoated name for jail—razor wire, locked doors, control officers, and a real threat of getting beat up.

Goshen was serious. It made me ask myself, "Where am I headed in life? To prison? I'm about to turn 18. I need to get my mind right so I can get out of here and succeed in life." After about a month in Goshen, I decided there was no point in fighting the system anymore.

I'd always heard the saying, "Fake it till you make it." A fellow resident at Goshen explained to me the benefits of faking the treatment: (1) people would trust me and let me have privileges, and (2) I might actually feel better.

In groups, I began to talk, thinking, "I'll give them what they want to hear." But I felt relieved once I started to speak about how I felt being away from home and stuck in jail, and how I felt knowing that my mother really didn't give a crap about me. As I talked, the residents and group leaders looked at me like they were seeing a ghost.

The group's topic every day was anger, which I didn't like, so I asked if we could bring up other topics. The group leader liked the idea, and from then on the group was open, which made it easier to talk. I started to talk about my feelings of abandonment, fear, and betrayal, and how my past affected me on a day-to-day basis. The group leader and my peers gave me a lot of support, and I began to trust them.

Letting out some of my emotions was the best thing I've done. It helped me find out who I was. It felt great to break my family's taboo against talking about our feelings or discussing what happened inside our house. Telling my secrets, I felt like I was rebelling. Pretty soon, you couldn't get me to shut up.

It's too bad it took me three years and the prospect of getting sentenced to an adult prison to open up. Once I did, I understood why St. Mary's and the judge wouldn't let me go home—I was a really angry guy, and going home to my family wouldn't help me.

Once I understood that my anger and my past were controlling me, I began to try to control my anger. I learned some methods to control my temper, like counting, deep breathing, or my personal favorite—pleasant imagery. (I'd think of the best-looking girl I knew and imagine locking lips with her. That always calmed me down.)

> **It's too bad it took me three years and the prospect of getting sentenced to an adult prison to open up. Once I did, I understood why St. Mary's and the judge wouldn't let me go home—I was a really angry guy, and going home to my family wouldn't help me.**

At Goshen, I also got into creative writing and poetry. Putting my experiences down on paper helped me fight my inner demons. Writing became my self-medicine.

Still, as with all recoveries, it was hard to change. At times, my anger got the best of me. In the facility, there were always guys playing too rough or bad-mouthing each other. In the past, if someone did that to me, I would have waited for the staff to open up the rec room and popped off without a thought.

I had to practice calling a time-out inside my head, counting to 10, or thinking about my best friend. I also learned to daze out when someone was talking to me in a way I found disrespectful. If someone started talking reckless, I stopped listening and stared into space. Or I'd walk away, put on my headphones, write some poetry, or draw pictures to focus on my own thoughts. All of those strategies helped calm me down.

When I turned 18, I had to leave Goshen. Things got real hectic because the courts didn't want me to go home but couldn't find a place for me to live. Then I got the answer to my prayers. A group home in Manhattan would take me in.

Before I left for Manhattan, some staff gave me some final tricks to handle my anger: they taught me how to knit and how to restrain people without hurting them. The knitting helps me feel calm when I'm by myself. The restraining comes in handy if someone's threatening me or hits me, and I don't want to hit them but feel nervous about just walking away.

I was delighted that I was finally free after almost five years. But along with my freedom came some great temptations.

Soon after getting out, I got back into smoking cigarettes and now I'm addicted again. I got caught up in the drug game as well, smoking weed, which I had always loved. Lots of guys in my group home smoked and I wanted everyone to like me and think I was cool. I also just wanted to get high. I love that giddy, spaced-out feeling weed gives me. It almost cost me my freedom, though.

Weed made my anger rise, and when I smoked, I didn't want to stop it. When I was high, I didn't care if I got locked up again. Soon I was fighting at least once a week, over stupid stuff like someone bumping into me. I also started robbing people to have money in my pocket, or because I felt angry just from being high.

The cycle kept repeating: Fight, weed, anger, fight, weed ... and so on. I had so much going for me but I almost blew my freedom on weed.

Finally, my probation officer did a drug test on me and I came up positive. He sent me to the Realization Center, a program that runs outpatient groups for people with drug problems.

The groups help me so much. We talk about how our drug problem is affecting our lives and how to stop the cravings. Now, after a few months, my cravings are down to a minimum and my anger is getting back in check. I haven't fought or smoked weed in three months.

I've gone back to my good habits—the daze-out, counting to 10, knitting, poetry, and creative writing.

I think keeping my anger under control is going to be a lifelong struggle. But at least now I'm focused on my future again. I don't want to give up my freedom for anything. I love it too much. When I want to fight or smoke weed, I remember how good it feels to walk to the corner store and buy a bag of chips whenever I want. The girls make freedom worthwhile, too, because in the facilities there were no females (besides the old staff). Plus, I have family that I don't want to lose again.

I've seen so many of my friends go back to jail. But I don't really fear I will end up doing more time. I've changed a lot, and I have too many people in my corner to lose this battle. A lot of staff have given me second chances and have put their faith in me. I hope I can make them proud.

KARATE KILLED THE MONSTER INSIDE ME

by Robin Chan

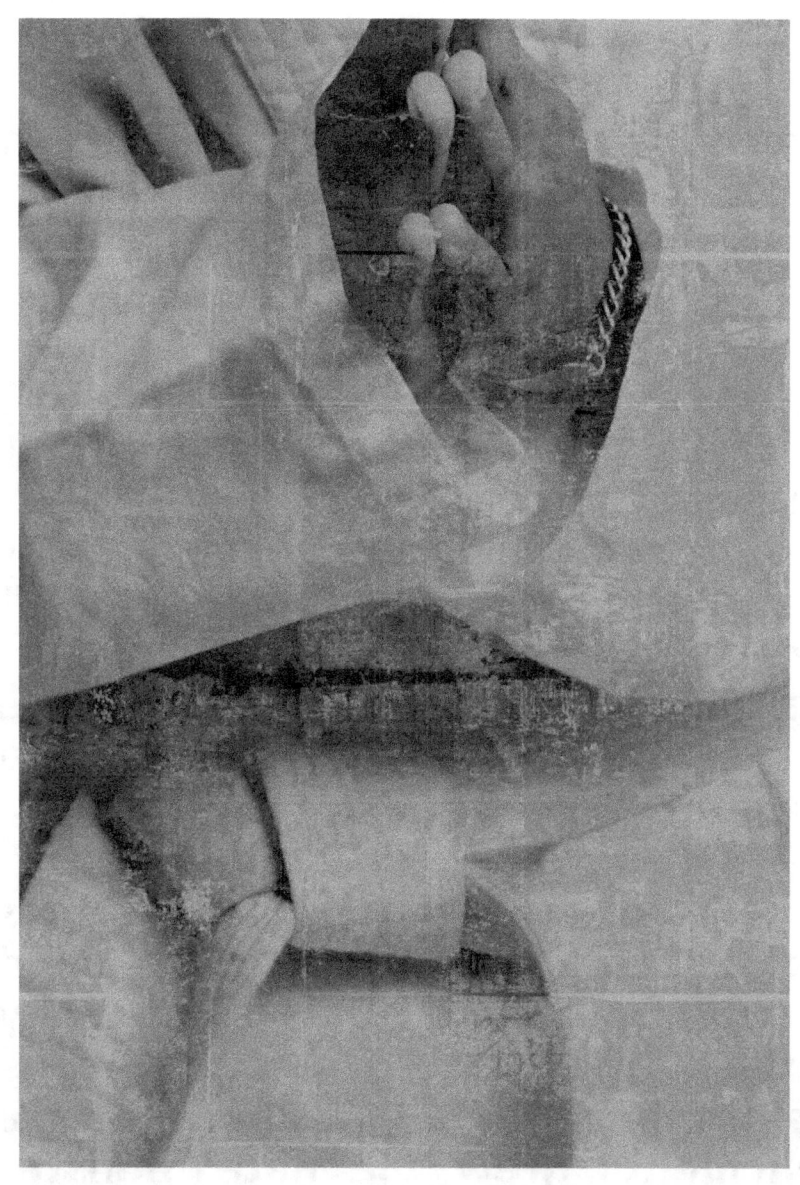

I was fed up. From the time I was 4 years old, I was teased and pushed around by bullies on my way home from school because I was short and frail-looking. My family and I also got harassed by racist punks because we were the only Asian people living in a white neighborhood.

These incidents grew the hate monster inside of me. Most days, I would come home from elementary school either angry or crying. My family and friends tried to comfort me, but I had been storing up the loads of anger inside me for too long. I thought I was going to explode.

> **From the time I was 4 years old, I was teased and pushed around by bullies on my way home from school because I was short and frail-looking. These incidents grew the hate monster inside of me.**

When I was about 9, I found the answer to my problems. I decided to learn karate so I could break the faces of all the people on my "hit list" (anyone who had ever bullied me or my family).

I started nagging my parents about learning karate. They agreed because they wanted me to build up my self-esteem, learn some discipline, and have more self-confidence. All I wanted was to learn the quickest way to break someone's neck, but I didn't tell that to my parents.

I was about 10 years old when I finally got my chance. My first dojo (that's what martial arts students call the place where they study and practice) was small, musky, and smelled lightly of sweat. The instructor, Mr. Sloan, was as strict as an army drill sergeant.

Mr. Sloan taught us how to do strange abdominal exercises that were like upside-down sit-ups and really difficult to do. He wouldn't allow any slacking off from people who got tired. It was only the first day, what did he want from us! I quickly discovered that I was really out of shape. Before the first lesson was over, I was already thinking about dropping out.

By the end of the second lesson, however, I had decided to stick with it. Mr. Sloan was teaching us cool techniques for breaking out of arm and wrist locks and that got me interested.

Mr. Sloan was a good instructor. Within a few months, my class of beginners went from learning the basic punch, block, and kick to learning a flying jump kick. He also taught us effective techniques for breaking out of headlocks and strangleholds. We enhanced our skills by sparring with each other and practicing at home.

Although the dojo had limited resources (there were no boards to break, no martial arts weapons, and no fighting gear), I still learned a lot and had a lot of fun. I became more flexible from the rigorous exercises. In addition to practicing our karate moves, we did pushups, sit-ups, and leg, arm, torso, and back stretches to limber up.

We also meditated together. Near the end of class, Mr. Sloan would "guide" us through the meditation by telling us to clear our minds. One time, he told us to picture ourselves breaking free of a barrier or knocking a barrel or a wall to pieces. He said that whenever we had problems or faced challenges that got us frustrated, we should go to a quiet place, relax, and close our eyes. In our minds, we should picture ourselves knocking over that problem or challenge. Mr. Sloan said that doing this should make us feel better. After meditating on "killing" the problem, he said, our minds would be clear and we'd be more determined to solve it.

> **Mr. Sloan made it clear that he was teaching us karate not just so we'd be able to kick someone's ass, but so each of us could become a role model—someone with a good conscience, good morals, self-respect, and respect for others.**

Mr. Sloan also made it clear that he was teaching us karate not just so we'd be able to kick someone's ass real good, but so each of us could become a role model. A role model, he explained, was someone with a good conscience, good morals, self-respect, and respect for others.

We worked on developing these qualities in class by bowing to the instructor, addressing him as "sir" or "sensai," treating fellow students with respect, and listening to our sensai's lectures, which taught us about respect, discipline, manners, and so on. We were taught to exercise these qualities not only in the dojo, but outside as well.

The goal of becoming a role model was a major factor in my wanting to continue to study karate. I no longer saw the martial arts as a way to get back at people who hurt me. I knew from experience that there were enough menacing and evil people in this world. I didn't want to become one of them.

After only a few months, I was much more confident and disciplined. I knew that I was now capable of protecting myself against enemies. Whether or not I chose to fight someone who bullied me was beside the point; I knew that I could knock them out. Just knowing that made me feel good about myself, so why fight when you're already ahead? Besides, not fighting would save my knuckles from a lot of pain.

> **I no longer saw martial arts as a way to get back at people who hurt me. I knew from experience that there were enough menacing and evil people in this world. I didn't want to become one of them.**

The insults and slurs I encountered did not bother me as much anymore. As a matter of fact, the discipline and basic philosophy I learned from karate held back the punches I was tempted to throw when people tried to provoke me to fight.

For example, one day when I was walking home from school, two teenage guys walked into me. One of them said, "Watch it, ch—" and shoved me. They started pushing me, but I just blocked their pathetic pushes. They weren't getting enough thrills from just shoving me, so they started cursing and spitting at me, too.

I started getting really aggravated. Then I remembered something Mr.

Sloan had told me when I asked him what to do when someone bothers you. "Lowlifes like these do not deserve the time and energy you put into punching them out," he said. "Just walk away and splash some cold water on your face."

I cooled down and started walking away. The two guys saw that I was not affected by their stupid remarks. I heard one of them say, "Forget that ch—, man."

It was ironic how I wanted to learn karate so that I could beat up people like these, and then, when I got the chance, I didn't go through with it. What karate taught me was that fighting isn't the right way to solve a problem. It just turns you into one of those lowlifes who don't have the conscience, respect, manners, or education to know how to handle their problems any other way.

> **What karate taught me was that fighting isn't the right way to solve a problem. It just turns you into one of those lowlifes who don't have the conscience, respect,**

> **manners, or education to know how to handle their problems any other way.**

I was good enough at karate by that point that it wouldn't have been a fair fight. But if I had given in to the temptation to beat up those guys, I would have felt ashamed and guilty. I would have disappointed Mr. Sloan, who taught me that the most important rule of karate is not to fight unless it's necessary for self-defense; my parents, who told me never to fight with anyone even if they are wrong; and myself, because I feel that it is wrong to take advantage of a situation.

The time and effort I was putting into karate was getting me worthwhile results. I used to be wild when I was with my friends, but I had become more reserved and well behaved. I also used to slack off in school but not anymore. I really started gearing up and hitting the books. My teachers and parents noticed the difference and were happy with what they saw.

I was even becoming a role model for some of my friends. They told me that they had never seen me work so hard before, and they admired the high grades I was earning in school. They decided to follow my example and started pulling their acts together and improving their grades.

Unfortunately, Mr. Sloan's class ran for only a year and when time was up, all of us were really upset. But our instructor had a new class of misfits to turn into the fine role models we had become.

Studying karate was a wonderful experience. I'm thankful to my extraordinary and deserving instructor, Mr. Sloan, and to my great family who let me go to the dojo and have supported me always. Together, Mr. Sloan and my parents have made me realize that I should always try my best and put a sincere effort into whatever I do. They have geared me up, morally and spiritually, to reach for the stars.

BUM-RUSHED BY THE PAST

by Natasha Santos

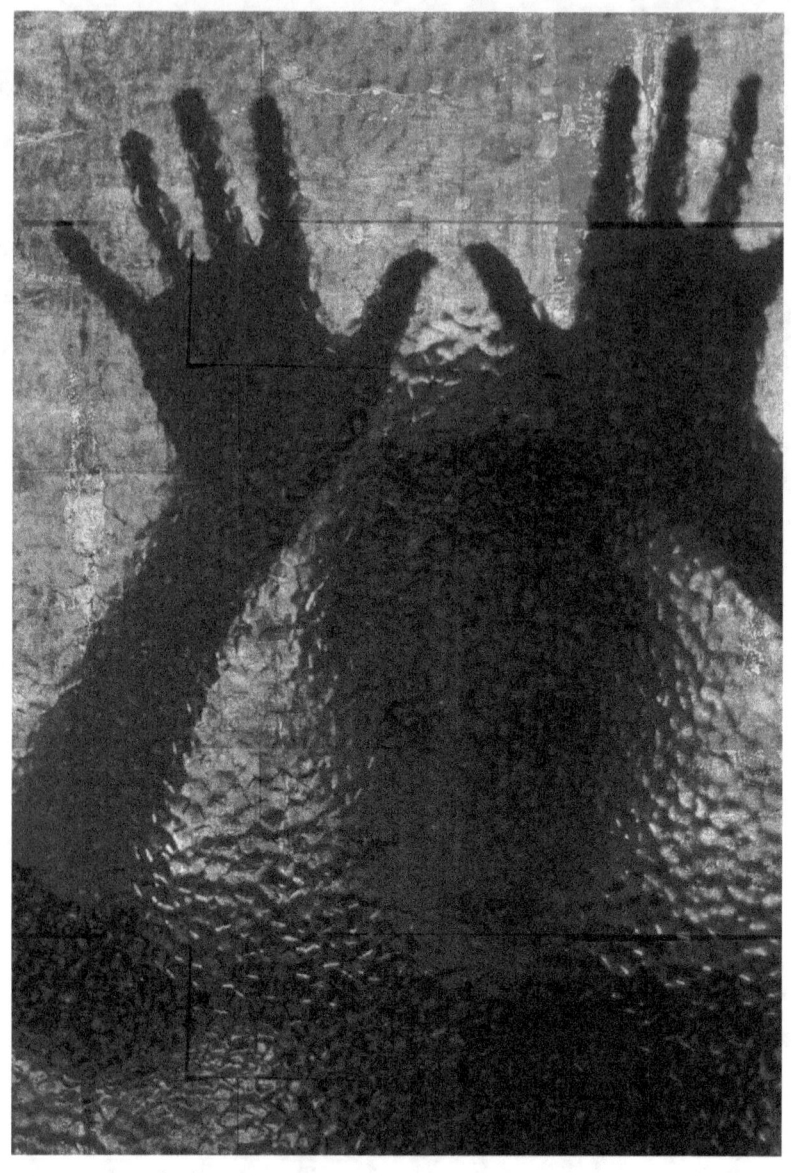

This is the story of a girl born in the projects, neglected by her parents, and tormented by memories of families she's no longer a part of. It's about how I spent six years in foster care and got adopted. It's not an easy story to tell. It leaves me feeling weak. But it's a story that I must tell so that I can move on.

Here's me in a nutshell: playful, strong-willed, and in control. I'm motivated in school, and voraciously competitive. Well, that's what people see anyway. Inside it's quite different. I'm angry, emotional. Mostly I feel weak.

When I was young, I showed my anger. I was a problem child. I tried to stab a girl with a pencil, yelled at the teacher, threw temper tantrums, and just walked out of the room. Then I moved. I wanted to change because nobody liked me when I acted like that, so I began to pretend to be a good girl, a happy girl. Now I've acted like this fictitious person for so long that I've literally forgotten how to be any other way.

But I still have this anger inside. I don't want to go back to the way I was as a child. I would feel too ashamed, like I was letting myself down. I also feel that if I'm so good at pretending to be someone outside, I should become that person inside. But I can't. This really ticks me off.

I don't want to be one person on the outside and a completely different person on the inside. So I am constantly trying to think of ways out of it. First I tried hiding my feelings. That didn't work. I only ended up with broken spirits and angry thoughts at night.

I also tried burying myself inside work, so as not to be stuck with myself. Inside my head was a mass of confusion and conflict that I didn't want to deal with, because I knew it would slow my life down.

I was afraid that if I let my "real" self out that I might be sad. I would be giving up the identity that I'd been building up for so long. That might cause new problems. I didn't know what to do, so I began to write.

> **It wasn't hard for me to understand why I have so much anger, shame, and sadness inside. It was just hard for me to open up and let it out.**

It wasn't hard for me to understand why I have so much anger, shame, and sadness inside. It was just hard for me to open up and let it out.

Growing up in my family, and then in foster care, gave me plenty to be upset about. My brother and sisters and I grew up in chaos. We looked atrocious. Our hair, while always braided, was knotty and full of lint. Our clothes were dirty and unkempt. We yelled at adults for reprimanding us. My sisters would come in at 11 at night without explanation. Multiply one missed curfew times seven, because that's how many kids lived in my house. We ranged from 4 to 13 years old.

People walked in and out as they pleased: Neighbors, friends, boyfriends, girlfriends, my brother's "business associates." My father was rarely around. My mother seemed depressed and isolated. She barely left the house or her bedroom. I didn't know it then but she was using drugs. Maybe that's why she failed to notice that when I visited family on vacations, my uncle sexually abused me.

The refrigerator was usually filled with air and peanut butter, and welfare checks went to silly items that didn't last, like donuts and sodas or the occasional doll for us to share. I woke up wondering how I would get something to eat. Would I dare wake my mother to ask her for money? No, it wasn't worth the beating.

I don't think that's a normal thing to worry about at age 6.

I didn't know what I was feeling back then. I just knew that something wasn't right. I would act up in school, lash out at my peers, and get in trouble a lot. I got detentions and suspensions, and when that didn't work the teachers gave up and ignored me. Once an aunt took me to her house for the weekend and I scratched up a man's car. Through all this, no one once asked me what was wrong.

For as long as I can remember I always wanted a traditional family. I wanted to see a mother's face that lit up a little when I walked in to the room. I wanted to see a proud father looking on as his daughter grew. Instead I saw a mother with a look of pure malice in her eyes, and a father with a face of stone neglect.

When the police came the first time, there was no adult and little food in the house. The police told my sister (who was 13 and babysitting us) that if that didn't change in 24 hours, they would come and take us. My mother came home and we told her what the police had said. (She didn't do anything. Surprise, surprise!)

The next day, almost the exact same thing happened, with my mother stuttering out quick replies to save her ass. "Look, officer, there's no food because we just moved here ... my furniture hasn't come in yet ... the heat hasn't been turned on yet."

"We moved in almost a year ago," I told the cops.

My first foster family lived in a house with a front and back yard. I wanted so much to be a real part of that family. But there was an invisible wall between us. In that home, my siblings and I were not included in family activities. We were treated, well, like foster children. Complete with our own set of plates and spoons.

In that house, I felt jealous and timid, as if I were beneath the family, as if the abuse I'd endured had left me impure. The way they treated me made me feel like a parasite, a leech sucking up the family's happiness. Then the mother left, and her daughter, Diane, moved into her house and became our foster mother. Her first act was to make my oldest sister leave.

When Diane took over, I had a feeling that I couldn't identify—a feeling somewhere in my body that something big had changed. Months later I finally figured it out: it was a sense that my new foster mother was a threat.

At first she turned her anger on other children in the home. But soon I became the target. In the years that followed, my foster mother labeled me a liar and a thief. I was rejected and isolated in a way that is indescribable.

I was being cursed at and accused of crimes I hadn't committed. Her attacks left me feeling worthless and with confidence issues I still face today.

    I didn't want to be there, but I feared that if I spoke up I would be sent someplace worse. So at school and on visits with my mother I would always laugh and happily agree with everyone. I kept an optimistic smile on my face while I was feeling the exact opposite. I wanted to be strong for the other people in my family, and I wanted to be accepted.

    But it didn't matter what I did. There was no love in my foster mother's heart for me. She didn't care. Diane decided to put me out of her house. Confused, frightened, and angry, I moved again.

    Living with different foster families changed my personality. I am still the smart, friendly, and accomplished person that I've always been, but over the years I gained something, like my fake perkiness, or lost something, like the gentle quietness I used to have. I thought changing myself was good because it made me okay to the people around me. But that calm is something I can't get back, and looking back, I'm angry at my "guardians" for allowing me to change.

About four years ago, I moved to a new home and, last year, my new family adopted me. That has been working out best for me. The family is close, religious, and moral. My mother is not the type to sugarcoat things, but she is patient with me and my ideas. If I get in trouble at school, she doesn't yell or curse at me. She speaks to me, and listens to what I have to say. No other "mother" has done that.

When I thought I'd finally found what I was looking for, I held back. I'd put my heart on my sleeve in my other foster homes and had it ripped out, so I kept my distance, not knowing how genuine their feelings were.

Feeling loved has given me a sense of security. That's allowed me to look back at the past. I've figured out that what I thought was normal in my other homes was actually abuse. I've realized that the way I was treated made

> **me feel intense anger, frustration, and fear of the world.**

I did some stuff that would have had me out of any other foster home in a heartbeat. I would break curfew, and do things they told me specifically not to do. Surprisingly, they understood my need to vent. That made me like them more.

A few months after I came to live with them, we had a Thanksgiving dinner. Only family had been invited. So I was confused when I found myself sitting next to my foster sister saying prayers. Were they not able to find a babysitter? After a while it began to sink in. They considered me part of their family. That made me feel what I hadn't felt in a long time: wanted.

Feeling loved has given me a sense of security. That's allowed me to look back at the past. I've figured out that what I thought was normal in my other homes was actually abuse. I've realized that the way I was treated made me feel intense anger, frustration, and fear of the world. Now that the abuse is over, I feel like I should be able to get over those feelings.

Yet I get the feeling sometimes that I've reached an invisible barrier, and that no matter how hard I try I cannot break it alone. How can I win the battle against fear and anger and move on to the next stage in my life?

This past year my emotions have been a roller coaster. In one day my feelings range from boredom to anxiety to anger to feeling like I'm going to cry. I think that's because I have my past on my mind all the time now. It's probably also because, this winter, my biological mom died. I wish I could've asked her why our lives had to be that way. Now I'll never get the chance.

My new awakening to the feelings and memories of my past is uncomfortable and makes it hard for me to concentrate in school. My grades show that. But the worst thing is that I've been having flashbacks and panic attacks. That's frightening.

When I panic, my head feels like it's going to burst open, I can't stop crying, I flash back and I shake, and I can't get warm. I don't know what else to do but let it happen.

When the panic attacks started a few months ago, I would shut myself in my room and go through it alone. I was afraid to explain what I was going through because I didn't want to be seen as crazy.

> **I get the feeling sometimes that I've reached an invisible barrier, and that no matter how hard I try I cannot break it alone. How can I win the battle against fear and anger and move on to the next stage in my life?**

Then, one Saturday not long ago, I went over to a friend's house. She and I had plans, but at the eleventh hour her mother suggested shopping. As 16-yearold girls we jumped at the chance. Her mother offered to give her daughter and niece $20 each and me $10. I felt excluded. The headache started. Just around my eyes.

In a cab to the mall, her niece began making comments about the smell in the car. I felt those comments were directed at me because the sexual abuse I endured left me feeling polluted, like my body was full of a contaminating poison. The headache got worse.

At the mall I couldn't find anything in my price range, so my friend's mother abruptly asked for her money back. I felt insignificant. I became dizzy. As we roamed around, her son began kicking and hitting me. I could not return the favor because he was only 2. Now I was feeling anxious.

We found another cab home, and her niece began singing, "When you wake up in the mornin' gotta wash." The 2-year-old began rubbing my face with his dirty, sticky hands. I told him to stop. His mother also told him to stop. Then she asked me what he was doing. I told her he was touching my face and his mother said I shouldn't mind because my face was already dirty. Then I couldn't see straight.

I had to go. Now. So when the cab reached my friend's house, I told her I had to leave and went home. As soon as I got into my bedroom I began to sob. Soon that turned into heart-wrenching crying. My body began to shake, my head throbbed, I was having trouble breathing, my chest was getting tighter, and I felt as if I were going to pass out at any moment. I was panicking.

I didn't know what to do. But this time I did know I couldn't go through it alone. I began to call people who I thought could help. First I tried calling the friend I had just left. Her mother picked up. No help.

Then I tried another friend. She wasn't home. Finally, with hesitations, I called my mother. She became angry, saying, "I can't do anything for you. What do you expect, I'm at work!" We hung up. I called back crying but she got angry and said I was talking nonsense. She hung up.

I called another friend. She was baffled. Then my mother called back, telling me, "Lie down. Relax and try to lie down." I tried. For about two hours I shook and cried, went hot and cold. My mind felt as if it wanted to drift into an abyss but my body couldn't relax.

I called my mother and finally she told me to come to her job. Half an hour later I was there. My mother immediately began telling me that bottling up all my feelings resulted in these panic attacks. "You need to let all your feelings out. By bottling it in, it's eating you away like a cancer," she said.

That panic attack lasted three petrifying hours. But this time was different. I had called my mother and asked her for help. Although she seemed a bit overwhelmed, in the end she came through completely. She understood that it feels like I'm being bum-rushed with feelings I never knew I had.

My mother has also put me in therapy. I hope it will help. Dealing with all this anger and anxiety has had its consequences. But not dealing is not an option anymore. This is the story of my past, but now I want to write the story of my future.

THE MONSTER INSIDE

by Griffin K.

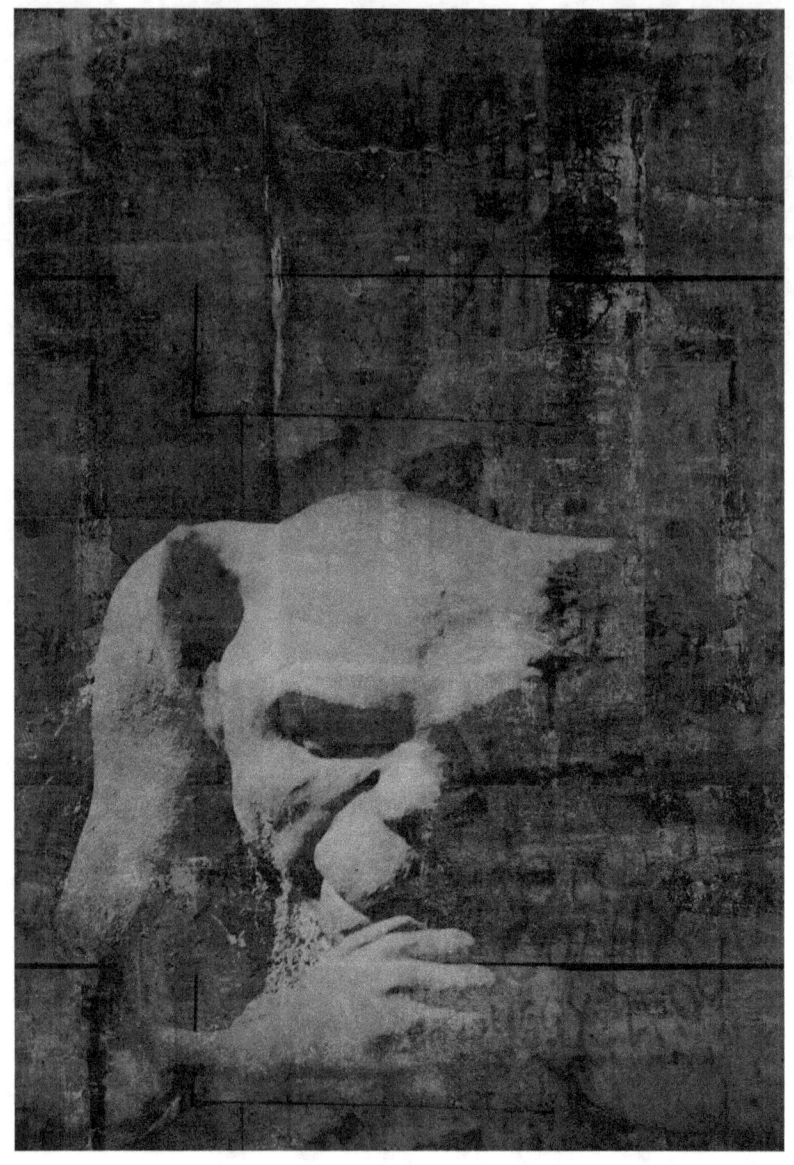

I've lived in eight different places. When I go somewhere new, I have one goal in mind: not to get into any fights. I always seem to fail at that goal, though. I'm not sure why. Everyone has a boiling point, right? My boiling point is low. After years of being abused by my father, and then stuck in residential treatment centers and group homes, I'm angry from the jump. So I flip and lose control.

> **I feel afraid of myself, of what I'm capable of. If I don't stop fighting, I won't be around much longer. I'll either be locked up or dead.**

In all the fights I've had, someone gets messed up, and it isn't me. I feel afraid of myself, of what I'm capable of. If I don't stop fighting, I won't be around much longer. I'll either be locked up or dead.

Last fall, I started at a new high school. I decided to handle myself differently, to just lie low. I was determined not to let history repeat itself. I told myself, "Sometimes it's cool to look soft. You know what you are, so why care about what someone else thinks about you? Do *you,* and don't stop."

My first day at my new school, I bumped into the dean. No lie, he seemed like a real cool dude. We kicked things off in the right way. He was telling me who to stay away from and who to be cool with. He pointed out the most troubled kid at that school, a kid I'll call the Big Bad Wolf. He was a tall blood, and real dumb, but thought he had no equal.

The dean said, "There are a lot of things in this school that you shouldn't get involved in." Then he showed me to my class, as if he had to protect me.

Not much later, I was playing ball and I had this guy David on my team. He was going nuts. This mother lover was not passing the ball for nothing. Damn near every shot he put up was a miss. Inside, I was burning. I hate playing with nuts, especially ones that don't score. Plus, the opposing team was led by the Big Bad Wolf. I felt I couldn't lose to the Big Bad Wolf in anything. I had to win, and David was messing all that up.

So I said, "Yo, David, pass the damn ball."

David did not say a thing. Then I said it again. The game continued with this fool not passing the mother-loving ball. I said, "Yo, David, you gonna pass that ball?"

He had the nerve to tell me, "Shut the #$&* up."

I told him the same thing. But by then it was too late. I had lost to the Big Bad Wolf. Then the Big Bad Wolf came over and said, "Yo, don't be talking to my boy like that. Do that again and I'll punch you in the face."

I looked him in the face and said, "Great ... whatever."

That's when the trouble began.

At first I stayed cool while they were messing with me, because I knew that if I were to retaliate I would have given them what they wanted—a fight. I did not want to fight. I don't get satisfaction from hurting people. But I was getting tired of getting messed with. And soon I had more than just a school problem. The Wolf Pack threatened me when I was in Harlem.

> **I did not want to fight. I don't get satisfaction from hurting people. But I was getting tired of getting messed with.**

I was chilling on my way back from a disappointing meeting with a friend. I was trying to relax and stay calm. I recognized one of the boys standing by a sneaker store from somewhere but I couldn't put my finger on it, so I walked into the store. Maybe 20 minutes later the same boy walked into the store and gave me the ill grill. If looks could kill I'd be dead.

So I left the store five minutes later. When I got outside, the Big Bad Wolf was right there. He said, "Get out my hood."

I just ignored him. But it seemed like just a matter of time before the Wolf Pack would have me at their dinner table. The trouble was getting way out of hand. So I decided to fall back, try to be myself again, lie low. I was doing well until I met Little Red Riding Hood.

One afternoon I was walking down the stairs at school when I saw Little Red Riding Hood crying like something devastating had happened. I stopped and asked, "What's wrong?" She looked at me with water in her eyes and said, "My brother died."

I started to talk to her slowly, cheering her up a little bit. Then I asked, "How did it happen?" Miss Hood looked like she was about to cry the Nile. She told me her brother had been shot in the head.

I felt her pain, every drip drop of it, like I was catching every tear that fell off Miss Hood's cheek. My own brother had been shot dead two years before. After that conversation, I started to grow feelings for Miss Hood. I feared that by caring about her I would show the Wolf Pack a weakness, but I didn't care.

Soon Miss Hood and I were having lunch and talking. The word got around school so fast I thought it was in the *New York Daily News.* One day, Miss Hood came to school looking very nice, and the Wolf Pack noticed a lot quicker than I did. As I made my way down the stairs, some kid handed me the news. "Yo, n—s downstairs just got finished throwing food all over Miss Hood. Son, you should have seen it, it was funny."

I thought, "These fools want war. They want to fight me, and messing with Miss Hood is their way of getting it."

For three more days I took a lot of crap. People were calling out my name, following me around the school. This was making me mad. Nobody calls out my name.

I told my guidance counselor I wanted a transfer. I already knew it was time for me to go. I told her three times that I wasn't safe in that school. I told her exactly how it would go down: I would fight, and I would be out before graduation. Somehow, after I told her, I thought she could handle the situation. But I myself did nothing but escalate the tension.

I started showing people a little bit of my strength. I'd go to the gym when the Wolf Pack was chillin' there. There was a punching bag there. I let out all the stress that I was feeling about them, punching the hell out of this punching bag. When people asked me if I was angry, I lied and said no.

Around this time, my foster mom and I were going through some drama. That stress was not helping me stay cool in school.

Then one Saturday I was kicked out of my foster mother's house and had to go back to a group home. I had to leave my baby sister, who was my world. I would have done anything for her, but I could not deal with my foster mother. It was not easy for me. I was in the Great Depression stage. That feeling only occurs when I'm in way over my head.

I came back to school the following Monday. That was something I regret doing. I should have taken a few days off, but I was only two credits from graduating and I needed to be in school. I was reading the newspaper when David walked into class—the same mother lover I had the beef with on the ball court.

I knew he was going to say something to me, and today wasn't the day. Something told me to walk out of the class and just continue reading the newspaper somewhere else, but my pride, my ego told me to stay, and that's exactly what I did.

I was reading about yesterday's game. I said, "A.I. got 36 points." I was saying something that should have stayed in my head.

David said, "That was yesterday's game."

I told David, "Mind your business."

David said, "Shut up before I punch you in the face."

I said, "Suck my %#&*."

David snatched the paper out of my hand and said, "Say that again and I'll punch you in the face." I said it again. Then I told him, "You don't know me. I'm not someone you want to mess with."

> **Something told me to walk out of the class and just continue reading the newspaper somewhere else, but my pride, my ego told**

> **me to stay, and that's exactly what I did.**

"You want to fight?"

Now I was tight. I knocked the newspaper out of his hand. I think David had no clue how much he had really pissed me off. Some teachers tried to stop us, but I was sick and tired of hearing this so-called gangster talk. I charged at David. I smelled fear all over him. I felt like a shark smelling blood.

David swung at me and he missed. Then he ducked. I had two choices: I could pound him out or I could go for the kill. I went for the kill. I didn't want to let him off easy. So I grabbed David by both sides of his ribcage and I started squeezing like there was no tomorrow.

I was sick of him and the Wolf Pack, of them messing with me and Miss Hood. I was sick of being messed with in general.

I heard David screaming. I was squeezing the life out of David, and I was smiling. I heard a teacher saying,

"Let him go," but the more I felt I was hurting David the more of my pain I put on him. Finally, they got me off him. When David left the classroom, he passed out. I felt nothing.

I was restrained until a police officer came. They put me in handcuffs and walked me out the door. They put me in the cop car. They gave me a summons and told me to be in court.

Not long after, I was in my first class of the day and this guy I didn't even know came and hit me on the back. That got me heated. I told him, "I'm not your friend. We ain't cool. Stop playing with me."

He said nothing. I assumed he took my warning, but nothing really goes as you wish it would. I was in the lunchroom when this other guy came up to me and said, "I'm going to make your life a living hell."

I said, "I'm already living in hell, but you're welcome to try."

He was tight. I could see it in his eyes. That was when I realized: They were not going to let me breathe. No matter how much I wanted to change, they weren't going to leave me alone. I had to get out of that school.

My counselor wasn't helping me. If I did it the official way it was going to take forever. So why not go out with a BANG!

I was late for gym class. So I jetted out of the lunchroom and up the stairs to the second floor. At the gym doors, guess who was on the other side messing with me? The same dude who had smacked me on the back earlier.

I said, "Yo, stop playing."

He was still standing in front of the doors, playing.

I told him, "Stop playing with me. I'm not the one."

He said, "Do you want to fight?"

I didn't answer the question. I attacked him. He hit me a few good times. Then I was choking him, like in slow motion, waiting for the gym staff to come and break up the fight. They weren't coming, so I punched him in the face. Then the staff came.

Now, as I sit back and think on what happened, I realize that I caused the situations. I ignored

> my feelings until they got to be too big, and I hurt two people.

The guards took me to the principal's office. They put the handcuffs on me and took me to their office. I sat and waited for the police officer to come and take me away again. At the police station I was caged for eight hours. It was fair. I did what I did and the school did what they needed to do.

When all this went down, I had no emotions. I felt those guys deserved what they got. I saw no way around it.

But it's been a year since then.

Now, as I sit back and think on what happened, I realize that I caused the situations. From the first day I stepped into that school, I felt the vibes. I had that feeling in my gut that I was not safe. I should have been pushing harder for a transfer. But I did nothing. I ignored my feelings until they got to be too big, and I hurt two people.

> Yes, I am kind, sweet, handsome, and intelligent, but I

> **have a dark side. I fear that my rage will be my downfall. My rage got me close to not seeing daylight ever again.**

Looking back, I feel that my actions were unacceptable. I wish I had backed down and taken my own advice to look soft.

When I think about how I had no feelings for so long, I feel like a monster, an animal. What happened in that school I will never forget. It scares me to this day how violently I reacted in those situations.

Yes, I am kind, sweet, handsome, and intelligent, but I have a dark side. I fear that my rage will be my downfall. My rage got me close to not seeing daylight ever again.

I know that I need to get under control. I don't want to hurt anyone anymore. Hurting gave me satisfaction at one point. It made me feel in control. It let my rage out. For a long time, hurting was the only way I knew how to feel like I would survive life.

When I look back, I see that I was always waiting for someone to intervene, someone to stop me—the teachers, my counselor, security, or the police. When I was hurting someone, I was looking around like a child, hoping someone would take control of the monster inside of me.

Now I realize I need to start depending on myself more. I need to feel control by controlling myself, not others. So now I'm back to the beginning. I'm trying to lie low again. I just hope I can take my own advice this time.

FINDING FREEDOM

by Valencia B.

"You going to grow up to be just like your mother and your father. Doing drugs, alcohol, no job, and getting locked up," my grandmother said. I was 11. I'd heard her say it so much that I started to believe it.

I started living with my grandmother at the age of 7. She put me down a lot. When I was in second grade, I got accepted to a gifted school, and she told me, "You can't go. How they going to let you into this school? You not smart enough."

Hearing her call me stupid hurt a lot. And as I got older, that hurt started to overwhelm me. She would tell me I was going to be a failure.

> **I started living with my grandmother at the age of 7. She put me down a lot. Hearing her call me stupid hurt a lot. And as I got older, that hurt started to overwhelm me. She would tell me I was going to be a failure.**

I felt blamed for everything that went wrong in the house. I wanted to tell my grandma off so bad but I knew it wasn't going to change her.

I felt as if no one understood me. I had so much pain in me that had to be released. Sometimes it hurt me so bad that I cut myself with scissors to take the pain away. Then I found another way to deal with the pain. I started to do exactly what she said I was going to do. And I felt free.

NOTHING BUT CRITICISM

"Valencia, wake up, that's all you do. Just sleep all day. Look at your room. It's dirty. You're so damned lazy. You know I'm going to court on Thursday. I'm going to have you out of here."

My grandmother didn't want custody of me. She often threatened to return me to the courts.

I didn't want to argue that day. So I got up and started doing what she asked. I got up out of bed and cleaned my room. I made sure it was spotless because I didn't want to get in an argument with her.

"Grandma, I'm going outside now," I said calmly.

"That's all you know how to do is run the streets. Why can't you stay in the house just for one day?"

Anger filled my head. I wanted to curse my grandmother out. Instead, I stormed out the door.

FIGHTING WAS MY RELEASE

Just outside my building, I heard, "Hi Valencia." It was my best friend, Mesha. She always made me laugh when I was mad. "Hey, where you going?" I asked.

"I was going to knock on your door," she said with a bright smile.

I just wanted to be happy and forget what had happened in my house. We went to go sit in the park.

A few minutes later, we saw some girls I had problems with. One of these girls and I had fought numerous times. It was always over petty stuff. Now they were walking toward us to start trouble again. I was tired of getting picked on.

"Hi," she said like she wasn't coming my way to start trouble.

"What's up," I said, real hard.

She started a petty argument, like I knew she would. As she got more disrespectful, I snapped. I jumped up, and with all of my power I punched her in the face. Then I kept on going at her. Mesha was trying hard to pull me off. But it was too late. The next thing I knew, the cops had pulled up, put handcuffs on me, and put me in the back of a squad car.

At the precinct, they asked me for my grandmother's number. I could already hear her words in my head: "You going to grow up to be just like your mother and father..."

They called her and put her on speaker phone. "Yes?" she said.

"This is the 41st Precinct calling you to tell you your granddaughter got into some trouble and the victim is pressing charges. She will be sent to juvenile detention tonight and you have to go to Family Court tomorrow morning."

"What's the charge?"

"Assault in the third degree."

"What time I have to be at court?" she asked.

SECOND CHANCES

The next morning, I awoke to a staff screaming, "WAKE UP, GOOD MORNING, RISE AND SHINE LADIES."

After breakfast, they took us downstairs to a big room where lots of kids sat handcuffed and in shackles, and soon I was, too. They told us all to stand up and make a straight line and they told me to come in the front. It was hard walking in those shackles. They hurt my ankles.

> **I started fighting everybody who I felt disrespected me. I felt undefeatable. It got out more pain and anger than cutting myself.**

I went in front of a judge named Robert Reed. He was nice. He let me out into a program instead of sending me to jail. I told him how I was going to follow rules, and I believed myself.

But once I hit my neighborhood, everything the judge said to me didn't matter. My old friends made me feel safe. I was free.

I started to fight even more. I was tired of getting bullied. Once I learned to fight real good, I started fighting everybody who I felt disrespected me. I felt undefeatable. It got out more pain and anger than cutting myself.

I got locked up several more times. Judge Reed kept letting me go because he believed in me. He believed I was going to grow up and be someone. But then I caught another case for shoplifting. This time I had a different judge and she was strict. "I'm going to let you back into the community this time, young lady, but if you violate probation, be prepared for a sentence."

Once again I said I wouldn't mess up, but once I hit my block, everything changed. I stopped doing the program they gave me, I didn't go to therapy, and I stopped going to probation.

My neighborhood is one of the most dangerous in the Bronx, but I had friends to protect me. Well, I called them my friends. And most of the teens were nice to me. They weren't mean like my grandma. I got so into them that I never wanted to leave their sight.

They started smoking weed so I started smoking. I stopped going to probation because my probation officer would give me a drug test. And I was fighting even more. It was like I was in a gang but I wasn't. On my block we just protected each other.

There was a warrant out for my arrest for violating probation and my grandmother turned me in. I was back in juvenile detention again. This time, I was getting sentenced.

STUCK ON NEGATIVE

They put me in an RTC (residential treatment center) called Graham Windham instead of a detention center. A detention center is more secure. You are told when to eat, sleep, and use the bathroom. You can't do anything without adult supervision or permission. An RTC is mostly for kids with behavioral problems. There are rules, but you are given more freedom.

When I first arrived, I was still fighting and I didn't pay attention in school. I didn't like all the rules. I thought I wasn't going to make it. I felt like nothing was going to change me.

I had low self-esteem. I thought I was the ugliest girl in the world. I mutilated myself. But Graham Windham changed the way I thought about myself.

There's a lot to do at Graham Windham. We went to school, and there were trips on the weekends, extracurricular activities, and jobs to keep us occupied. We had talent shows in front of the whole campus. All these activities helped us stay focused, out of trouble, and away from negativity.

> **People at Graham Windham taught me to have respect for myself. They told me that if I had attitude and disrespected people, nobody would respect me.**

When I got to Graham Windham all the negative messages my grandmother had given me and all the negative experiences I'd been through were stuck in my head. All I could remember were the bad times. It made me hate myself. I wanted to fix the way I felt about myself, but I didn't believe I could.

People at Graham Windham taught me to have respect for myself. They told me that if I had attitude and disrespected people, nobody would respect me.

OPENING UP

What really helped me was something called Girls' Group. In these groups we'd all sit in the living room in a circle and tell our stories. The staff would hardly say anything. They would just listen to us talk to each other.

A lot of the girls in there went through even worse things than me. Some of their parents left them at a young age and never came back and they went into foster care. Some of them had been abused. One of the girls was a crack baby, and her mom kept telling her she should have thrown her in front of a car.

All of the stories were sad. Everyone cried and everyone listened. Some of the girls felt like they had gone wrong so much. I think they felt, as I did, that they could never change.

The first time I opened up to others was when the other girls were telling me how bad I was in the cottage and how I was making their cottage go bad.

One of the girls said, "Valencia, you need to work on your anger and the fighting. They won't hesitate to lock you back up. I don't want to see a pretty girl getting locked back up into a horrible place for not doing something that should be easy. Just focus on yourself and try to change your ways. And don't forget, you can always come to me and talk."

That was the first time someone my age had said something like that to me. I thought, if she believes she can help me, that means I really need to change. She spoke to me like she cared, and she didn't want to see me fail. I felt like that was a true friend, so I took her advice. I started talking to her instead of fighting so much.

I FINALLY FELT ACCEPTED

Soon I was able to share with the entire group. I was getting better and better. And I was proud of myself. I learned how to choose friends who accepted me for who I was.

Speaking about my feelings started to take away my pain. I was comfortable expressing myself around a group of teens with problems like mine. I didn't want to keep doing the negative things. I wanted to stop. The other girls made me believe I could because they had. And every time I saw someone leave happy because they felt like they were a new person, it made me stronger.

When I was upset and wanted to destroy things, I would go talk to one of the other girls to help me calm down. I learned coping skills, like how to walk away from problems when I'm about to get upset. The girls told me that if my grandma says something upsetting I should take a couple of breaths and tell her, nice and calm, that I didn't think it was right what she said to me. If she kept on, I could tell her nicely, "I don't want to get upset" and walk away.

Every time we had this group it encouraged me more to change the old me and make a brand-new person. Everyone in the group helped each other grow.

LETTING IT GO

Now I'm living with my dad. He doesn't trust me yet. When I do something wrong he says I haven't changed at all and that I'm going to end up back in jail. But I don't get mad and start stressing because I know I'm way different from how I used to be. Instead of talking back, I walk away. And if I get angry I write, listen to music, or take a walk.

My grandma still acts the way she used to, but I'm not going to let her get me mad anymore. And I feel the same way about everyone else who puts me down. Now when people say cruel things to me, I look at them and I say to myself, "Maybe they are going through stuff and they don't know how to express themselves like me. Or maybe they have nothing better to do."

When I feel mad I try to remember, everything that comes to thought doesn't have to come to voice or action. When I feel like I want to fight, I remember that you get more with the positive than you do with the negative.

These experiences from Graham Windham helped me walk away from negativity and be proud that I'm doing it. I see my future now: a bright girl accomplishing her dreams.

I want to be a singer, a poet, and a psychologist. I want to write songs and poems to let people know how far I've come. It was hard for me to say what I wanted to be when I was younger, but now I see clearly. And I see a girl who feels truly free and unafraid of the world.

INVISIBLE MAN

by Onician Wood

My father left before I was born, leaving my mother to be a single parent, and me to be plagued with a feeling of abandonment. I felt shortchanged and hated that he wasn't there to pick me up when I fell down or congratulate me at my graduations.

As a teenager, I had bitter moments where the words "f— you" echoed in my mind whenever I thought about him. I flat out hated the man. Sometimes I blamed him for the difficult times I went through. I grew up thinking that they might've been easier had he been there for me.

According to my mother's younger sister Renee, my mother and father broke up because my mother discovered he was cheating. After their separation, my mother learned that she was pregnant with me. My father found out that she was expecting but didn't take responsibility for his actions.

GRANDPARENTS GAVE SUPPORT

My mother was petrified of telling her parents because my grandfather was a minister, and according to the Bible, having a child out of wedlock is a sin.

But on Christmas Day in the year before I was born, my mother revealed her secret to Aunt Renee. My mother lived in Nashville, Tennessee, and Aunt Renee was visiting her for the holidays from New York City, where she lived.

Renee soon announced to my grandparents that my mother was pregnant because my mother was too scared to tell them herself. But despite my mother's fears, after I was born, they gave me their unconditional love without turning their backs on me because I was an illegitimate child.

MOTHER DIAGNOSED WITH LUPUS

But hard times were coming. A year after my birth, my mother was diagnosed with lupus. Lupus is a disease where the immune system attacks the body tissue for unknown reasons. The disease took a toll on my mother. She was in and out of the hospital and constantly going to the doctor.

My mother was an art professor at Tennessee State University and worked long hours doing lectures and lesson plans. Due to my mother's job and endless doctor appointments, my grandparents babysat me a lot. So did my uncle, who lived with my mother, grandparents, and me.

My uncle didn't get along with my mother. They argued frequently, bickering over petty things. Sometimes I saw my uncle push her. But when she needed him to look after me, he came through.

UNCLE EASED FEELINGS OF ABANDONMENT

My uncle was the closest person I ever had to a father. He treated me like I was his own child, which eased my feelings of abandonment. My uncle taught me many things about being a man, instilling in me many of the ethics I have today. He told me never to call women names like b— and never to hit them.

> **My uncle was the closest person I ever had to a father. He treated me like I was his own child, which eased my feelings of abandonment. My uncle taught me many things about being a man, instilling in me many of the ethics I have today.**

But my uncle had ways that stopped me from idolizing him. Besides him shoving my mother and their constant verbal jousts, he was an alcoholic. His drinking scared me because most of the fights he had with my mother were when he was intoxicated. And sometimes he drank while driving.

Others told me that drinking was bad and could cause car accidents, among other things. My uncle had already been in a minor car accident, and I often worried that he would get in another one because of his drinking and driving. I learned from his mistakes, which is why I don't drink, do drugs, or push or hit women.

PLAYED FOOTBALL BY MYSELF

Though my uncle spent countless hours with me, he also had a child of his own, a marriage, and a job to tend to, so he couldn't be there for me all the time. And though my grandparents were home most of the time to watch me, they were too old to play with me in the front yard.

So I ended up playing games like football by myself. I felt so lonely. I threw the football as high as I could into the air and then sprinted across the yard to catch it, leaping to catch the ball, but in the end, never making it there in time.

I taught myself everything I know about sports by reading books or by observing the pros play. I even taught myself how to ride a bike while constantly falling off of it and crashing into mailboxes, fences, and parked cars.

It was not only painful physically, but emotionally as well, because sports and learning how to ride a bike are things I felt a father should teach his child.

LOSING MY MOTHER

When I was 4 or 5, my mother took me to the park on weekends and I saw kids playing with their fathers. I played by myself because my mother was exhausted from her illness.

> **That's when the feeling of abandonment hit me. There I was, throwing a football to myself while another kid was tossing the pigskin around with his pops. My resentment toward my father flared.**

That's when the feeling of abandonment hit me. There I was, throwing a football to myself while another kid was tossing the pigskin around with his pops. My resentment toward my father flared.

When I was 8, my mother's illness took a turn for the worse. We were walking back to the car after a lecture we attended and she had a seizure. The ambulance rushed her to the emergency room. She was put in intensive care.

Eight months after she had the seizure, still in the hospital, she died. I felt like part of me died with her. She awarded guardianship of me to Aunt Renee in New York.

MOVING TO NEW YORK

When my aunt was putting me in the car to drive to the airport, I kicked and screamed because I didn't want to leave my family and friends. After I got to New York, she enrolled me in Brooklyn Friends School, a Quaker private school.

I had the new kid blues. I was shy and felt like a social outcast despite the warm welcome my class gave me. I had a southern accent and some of the kids treated me differently because they saw me as country.

But when people discovered that I was good in sports, everybody wanted me on their team. If not for that, I probably never would've fit in.

When my classmates asked me about my parents, I told them, "My mother died from lupus when I was 8, and my father ... he ... he left before I was born." I felt like I was the special kid.

They said things like, "I don't know what I'd do without my mother" or asked me questions about how I got by without my father.

TREATED LIKE I WAS DISADVANTAGED

Most of the kids in the school knew their fathers, which made my feeling of being an outcast increase. I saw myself as a normal kid, but some people treated me like I was disadvantaged because I didn't have a father and had lost my mother.

They let me go ahead of them in line to get a snack or shoot first when we played the basketball game Around the World, saying, "Oh, let Onician go first. He doesn't have a father."

And when people mentioned parents or fathers, they became cautious around me. Some kids said, "Oh, I'm sorry, I forgot you don't have a father." When people kept asking me about my father or apologizing, it really got to me.

KNEW NOTHING ABOUT FATHER

I felt like I was the only one in the world who didn't have his father in his life. But I tucked that feeling deep inside myself, never talking about it.

I didn't feel as bad when they asked about my mother because I had memories of her. But my father was like French: foreign to me. I didn't know anything about him.

I didn't know where his side of the family was from or if he had other kids. Questions ranging from "What does he look like?" to "What is he like?" sailed in my mind, leaving me shipwrecked in uncertainty about not only who he was, but who I was.

I left Brooklyn Friends School after sixth grade and entered a Catholic school in Brooklyn Heights called St. Charles Borromeo. Even after I left elementary school, that feeling of being the only child without a father didn't leave me. But it did simmer down because people at St. Charles didn't make a big deal out of me not having a father and didn't ask about it so much.

A BOOK OF FATHERLY ADVICE

The feeling finally faded when I started ninth grade at Unity High School. I met kids who didn't know their fathers or were abandoned by them. I'd thought not feeling like the only kid without his father would comfort me.

But after I saw how many people there were without fathers, I was disturbed. I realized that absent fathers in the black community is a major problem. It's right up there with AIDS, poverty, and violence. But I didn't talk to any of my peers about it because I was shy.

Then, when I was 15, I read a book given to me by my best friend's mother, Dr. Doyle. The book, *Positive Messages: For Young Men Growing Up Without Their Fathers,* is by Marc Anthony Butcher and has short passages of fatherly advice. After finishing the book, I felt like I'd received some life guidance. I also decided to do a book report on it for class.

Dr. Doyle knew Mr. Butcher. So I called him to ask if he could come to my English class for my project and he agreed. After he spoke, people in class started to talk about not having their fathers and how it affected them. I found out that others felt like I did. I felt enlightened.

After class, Mr. Butcher and I had an extensive conversation about how we grew up without our fathers and what that meant for us.

I felt relieved to finally speak to someone about this problem. Since then, Mr. Butcher and I have become closer and talk on the phone whenever time allows.

DEALT WITH MY ANGER

A few months after talking to Mr. Butcher, I started analyzing my feelings toward the man I referred to as a figment of a father. I knew there was a lot of anger inside me, but I hadn't addressed it.

Anger and hate are like termites. They start eating away at you, destroying your happiness and causing you to become cold. Sometimes when I looked in the mirror, I could see this heartless person start to emerge.

I realized the animosity I felt toward him was only harmful to myself, and he wasn't feeling a drop of the pain I had inside. There was no use in hating him because he's my father. And in a backward way, he's had the biggest impact on my view of life.

STRONGER WITHOUT DAD

I set standards for myself to rebel against what he represents to me, which is a deadbeat, a coward, a cheater, and other words I'm not privileged enough to say in this article.

One of the biggest rules I've laid down for myself is that I won't have sex with a woman I don't love or wouldn't consider marrying. If anything happens and the girl gets pregnant, I want to be able to say that she's someone who I want to raise my child with.

> **Anger and hate are like termites. They start eating away at you, destroying your happiness and causing you to become cold. Sometimes when I looked in the mirror, I could see this heartless person start to emerge.**

Another rule is that I'll always be faithful to the woman I'm with because I never want to put another woman through the same thing my mother went through, no matter how attractive the other person is. It's more than a matter of being true to the woman—it's also being respectful to her, which is part of what my uncle taught me.

Now when I reflect back on my childhood and adolescence without my father, I realize that maybe it's for the best that he wasn't there. Though I felt I needed him sometimes, I don't believe he would've filled the shoes of what a father should be based on how he handled my mother's pregnancy.

By not having him in my life, I became a stronger person, adopting a perspective on life that makes me strive to be someone who's thoughtful and caring.

WRESTLING WITH MY ANGER

by Shateek Palmer

I was 9 years old when my grandmother died and I was taken from my family by ACS (New York City's Children's Services). I felt like I was the only person in the world; I didn't want to talk to anybody. ACS placed me in a foster home on the west side of Harlem in Manhattan.

I got into a lot of trouble in school because I wasn't able to control my anger. I was mad at the world because my grandmother had died and I'd been taken away from my family. After a month in the foster home, my sister and I were placed with my great-aunt Stacey. She lived in Roosevelt Island, which is between Manhattan and Queens. I liked it there, but I still got into trouble.

Aunt Stacey signed me up for the school near her. I didn't want to go because I worried I was just going to get in trouble like I did in my other school. I was in the fourth grade and I wasn't talking to anybody. My teacher tried to make me talk, but I didn't. I was on the basketball team, but I got kicked off because of my behavior in school.

> **When my grandmother died and I was taken from my family, I felt like I was the only person in the world; I didn't want to talk to anybody. I got into a lot of trouble in school because I wasn't able to control my anger. I was mad at the world.**

After that my gym teacher, Mr. Luce, asked me if I would like to join the wrestling team. I said no, but he kept asking. I kept saying no until he called my aunt and told her he wanted me in wrestling. He said he could see the anger in me, and he wanted me to use that anger in a positive way.

When I found out that Mr. Luce had called my aunt I felt that I was being forced into something I didn't want to do. I had in my head that wrestling was gay because of the singlets they had to wear (tight one-piece uniforms) and it was boys on top of boys. But my aunt said she also wanted me to wrestle to use my anger another way and hopefully stay out of trouble. I finally came to my senses and became a member of the wrestling team.

THE NEW KID

Practice was every day from 3 to 5p.m. The first time I went it smelled like gym socks and sweaty underwear and was as loud as a music concert. I felt like a lonely boat trapped at sea because everybody knew each other and I was just the new kid.

Mr. Luce seemed nice until wrestling practice started. Then he yelled and made us run nonstop for 30 minutes. Then we did push-ups, sit-ups, and pull-ups, and practiced moves on a partner. It was really hard and I wasn't good at wrestling. I tried to act tough, but I was really scared inside.

When you first start to wrestle, you feel like a practice dummy because you don't know the moves the other person is doing. The first move I learned was the headlock, and it took me a couple of weeks to learn it. When you learn a move in wrestling practice, you don't just do it once and you're done; you have to work on the move to get it down pat.

Our first team wrestling match was only four weeks after I joined the team. I was asked to wrestle at 86 pounds, a low weight for our team. That made me happy because you're more likely to win in a lower weight class.

But then I saw the person I was going against. He was tall, and his muscles were unbelievable. He looked fast—and he was. I was pinned in 35 seconds, and I began to cry right after. My teammates laughed at me.

TRAINING TO WIN

I promised myself that the next time we went against that team, I was going to kick that guy's butt. I learned from my teammates and from Mr. Luce. I got better at wrestling by working on every move every day for hours. I went to practice in the morning, during lunch, and also after school. I ate better meals and drank a lot of water and milk. I watched YouTube videos of Olympic wrestlers such as Terry Brands and John Smith.

About a month later we faced that team again, and I had to wrestle the same boy. I walked to the mat with "positive win" running through my head. My coach and my teammates helped me by telling me never to give up and never to show I was scared. But I was a little scared because this guy had beaten me before.

> **My strategy was to get mad by thinking about my grandmother's death and then use my anger to win my match. My grandmother was like the mother I always wanted. My real mother walked in and out of my life and put my grandmother through hell. Thinking about my grandmother leads me to my anger at my mother.**

When we got to the mat, I started thinking about getting taken away from my family and when my grandmother died. My strategy was to get mad by thinking about my grandmother's death and then use my anger to win my match. My grandmother was like the mother I always wanted. My real mother walked in and out of my life and put my grandmother through hell. Thinking about my grandmother leads me to my anger at my mother.

My opponent tried to do the move he beat me with the last time, but it wasn't working. I smiled at him, then I flipped him onto the end of the mat and gained two points. I could have finished him there, but I let him get up. Then I ankle-picked him and gained two more points.

I started to laugh at him. I started to think about my grandmother and my mother and felt like I could kill someone. When you wrestle it feels like you and your opponent are the only two people in the world. You're fighting for your life; you have to win the match.

Then I put him in a headlock and pinned him. Before I walked off the mat I shook my head at the other team and then the crowd started to say my name. The match was over and everybody yelled because I won my first match of the year. I walked off the mat with a smile on my face. All the applause seemed like a big reward.

TO THE CITY FINALS

My wrestling career was good for the next four years. Mr. Luce stayed my coach through fifth, sixth, seventh, and eighth grades. In all those years, I only lost twice and I kept getting better. I also didn't get in that much trouble because I started to really like wrestling, and if I got in trouble I wouldn't be able to wrestle. So I just focused on wrestling and school and became less mad at the world.

In eighth grade, I started to compete on a higher level. I got to the finals of the New York City championship; the bout (match) was at Hunter College on my 13th birthday.

The gym had so many lights it seemed like I was in heaven. So many people were yelling, including my cousins. They came to cheer me on, and that made me really happy.

My opponent's name was Paul. I heard my coach talking about what a tough wrestler he was. A little before the match started, Paul and his father came up to me and introduced themselves. His father said, "You and my son Paul are the best wrestlers in the city in your weight class; I'm glad to see you guys wrestling for the championship." Paul was really friendly to me throughout the whole championship. He shared his candy and we talked a lot until our match.

Wrestling matches are divided into three short periods. In the third period, I was losing by five points. I was about to give up when Mr. Luce called time-out. We walked to the bench and he told me to sit down. He seemed mad but glad at the same time. I was scared he was going to yell at me, but he didn't. He just talked to me calmly.

He said, "I know you want this. It's not going to be given to you. You have to take it. I know you don't want to think about this, but think about your past and get mad! Use your anger in the match. I asked you to be on the team because I know you have a future in wrestling. Now go win the match!"

FROM ANGER TO PRIDE

I walked onto the mat with a mad face on and my teammates started to cheer. They said, "Shateek, you can beat this guy. Put your mind to it!" I started feeling like the wrestling team was becoming my new family.

Paul and I stepped into the center of the mat and shook hands. I started circling him, then hit him with a single leg. Paul hit the mat and I got right on top of him—two points. I let him up and then got him into a headlock. I went for the pin but he got out.

With just 50 seconds left in the match, I was down by two points. Paul started to run around the mat so I couldn't get him until I finally tripped him and had him on his back. The crowd started to yell. Now I was winning because I got points for keeping him down on his back. "5, 4, 3, 2, 1, 0," yelled the crowd. The clock ran out, and I was the city champion. I jumped so high it seemed like I could reach the clouds. The whole team got together and yelled, "ONE TEAM! ONE WORLD! TEAMMATES FOR LIFE!"

"What did I tell you? You won!" said Mr. Luce. My teammates and I got dressed, then went out to eat pizza. Then we all took the F train home to Roosevelt Island.

"Aunt Stacey, I won the city championship!" I yelled when I got home.

"Shateek, I'm so proud of you. Later we are going to go out to eat," said Aunt Stacey. I was so happy.

> **For the first time in my life I completed a goal that I worked hard on. It made me feel like I could do anything with my life if I put my mind to it. Wrestling taught me how to control my anger on and off the mat, and I was happy I could fight without getting in trouble for it.**

I kept winning matches. I became a three-time city champion, a fifth-place winner at the state finals upstate, and a runner-up at the national championship. For the first time in my life I completed a goal that I worked hard on. It made me feel like I could do anything with my life if I put my mind to it.

Wrestling taught me how to control my anger on and off the mat, and I was happy I could fight without getting in trouble for it. After I started winning, people from all over kept saying, "You have a great future ahead of you. Keep up the good work." I believe that wrestling can take me far, including to college.

ESCAPING THE PRISON OF ANGER

by Tiffany H.

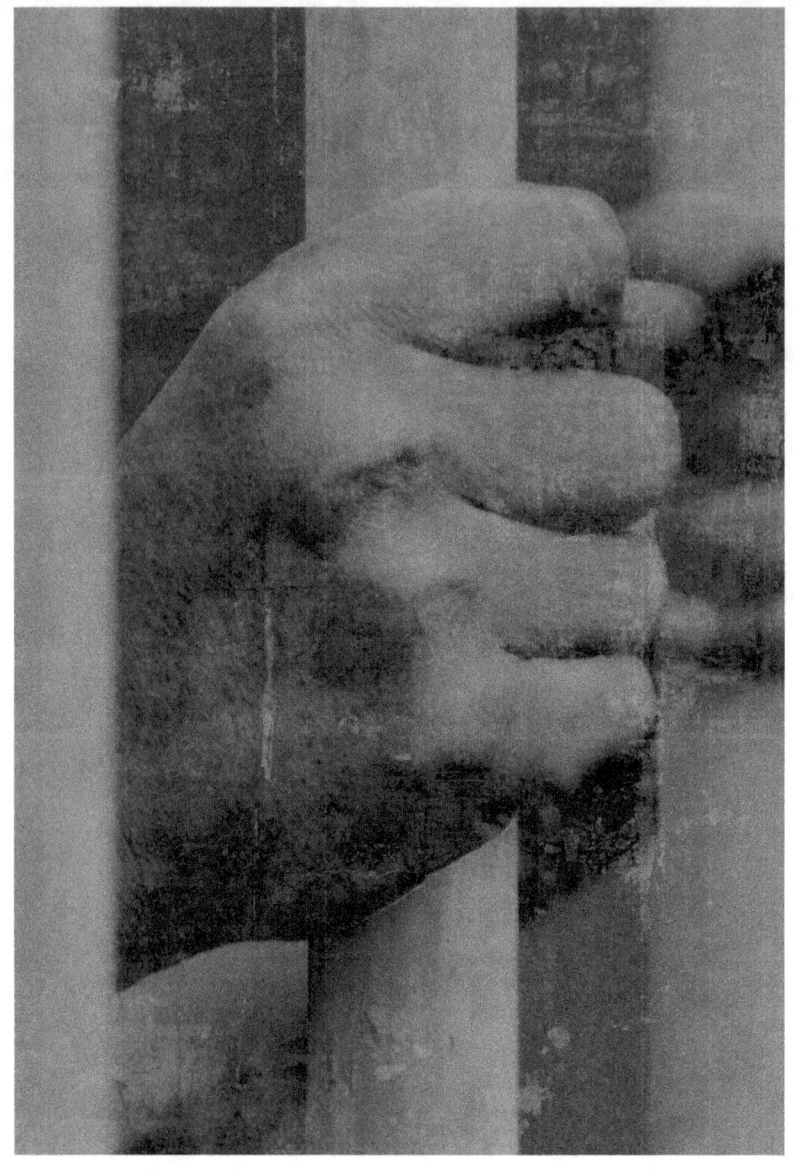

I haven't always been the nicest person. I used to scream at and hit my adoptive mom, and I didn't get along with most people. Thinking about how angry I was back then is scary. Now I handle things in a much healthier and happier way.

When I was a baby I was taken from my mother because she abused alcohol and lived on the streets or with random guys. She couldn't take care of me. I was put in care and had lived in five foster homes by the time I was 6 years old.

My longest placement was with a woman named Lori, who I stayed with for about four years. One day my social worker came to pick me up. She told me I was moving to another foster home to be with my little brother. I was hurt, angry, and scared. I loved Lori. I didn't understand that she wasn't my real mom. I'd lived most of my life with her and I didn't want to leave.

I think that's when I realized I had to take care of myself. I couldn't count on anyone to take care of me. No one could be my parents.

I went to live with my brother's foster mother. During the year I lived there, one of her relatives sexually and physically abused me. He told me, "This is between us, and if you say anything you won't have a brother and a family." So I didn't tell anyone. But at a court hearing to check on how things were going, I did tell a judge that I hated living there. We were moved to a new foster home that day.

A few months later, when I was 6, my brother and I started visiting a couple who wanted to adopt us. We would visit them on weekends. I liked them and the idea of being a part of their family. My brother and I moved out of our foster home and in with them a few months later. My brother and I called them "Mom and Dad." My mom would read nursery rhymes to me before bedtime. We would say a prayer and she would say, "Good night, buenas noches." We did things as a family, like game night. This was the first time that I felt like I was someone's child.

REMEMBERING BROKEN PROMISES

But even after they went to court to make the adoption official, I still felt that I would end up moving again. Promises had been made to me before. Lori told me I could live with her forever. Why would this be any different?

Although I felt welcomed at home, I was constantly battling my mom. I'd get upset over little things. My mom would tell me to do my homework, clean my room, or brush my teeth, and I'd go off and yell at her. Sometimes my mom would have to hold me down until I was calm. Other times I would explode—yell, bite, hit, kick, anything I could do to let out my anger. I wouldn't stop until I'd completely exhausted myself.

It wasn't like my mom was trying to hurt me, or forcing me to do something awful. I was just angry that she was telling me what to do. I was always angry, but I wasn't able to talk about how I felt. It had to come out somehow, and fighting was the only way I knew. My mom tried to help me by putting me in therapy, but it didn't work. I didn't like talking to the therapist, so my mom did all the talking.

> **I was always angry, but I wasn't able to talk about how I felt. It had to come out somehow, and fighting was the only way I knew.**

My behavior didn't change, so when I was 11 years old, I was sent to an all-girls therapeutic treatment facility near Denver, Colorado, called Excelsior Youth Center. I knew I was there because my behavior was out of control, but at the time I didn't think I belonged there. I thought being sent away was extreme, and I felt as if my mom was giving up on me. I didn't understand at the time how hard it was to live with me.

They told me I'd be there six months to a year, but I ended up staying three and a half years.

When I got there I met one of the staff, Jim, who took me to meet all the kids I'd be living with. They said, "Oh, you're Tiffany! We've been expecting you!" I was surprised because I did not expect everyone to be so nice to me. I thought they'd be mean because it was a treatment facility for kids with behavioral problems. This one girl came up to me and introduced herself. She told me her name was Ariel and that she was from Redondo Beach, California, like I was. It made me smile because I had only been there for a few minutes and I already had something in common with another kid.

After a few weeks of living at Excelsior, I didn't really miss home. I talked to my mom twice a week and went home every few months.

"I DON'T GO HOME AND FORGET"

Even though I'd left home, I didn't leave my problems there. I still didn't like being told what to do. I was always arguing and I would push limits to see how much the adult staff would put up with before I got into trouble.

At Excelsior there were harsh consequences when I didn't do what I was told. I got in trouble two or three times a week for talking during class or not sitting at my desk. I'd get sent to detention or put in time-out where I'd have to sit in a room by myself.

I think what helped most about time-outs was that there would usually be at least one staff around who I liked. They would say things to me like, "It's not like I don't care about you. I don't go home and forget about you guys." They'd share their own experiences, or they would just listen to me. I would tell them what upset me. When someone listened to me, I didn't feel ignored and I was less likely to be difficult at that moment. The punishments didn't keep me from acting out again, but I usually got something out of talking to someone.

> **When someone listened to me, I didn't feel ignored and I was less likely to be difficult at that moment. The punishments didn't**

> **keep me from acting out again, but I usually got something out of talking to someone.**

Another thing that helped me was the girls. Excelsior was the first place I made real friends. When I would get upset, sometimes I would talk to some of the girls and they seemed to understand. One time I was mad and I was roaming the grounds without permission. When I came back, some of the girls came up to me and said they were disappointed that I'd left and were worried and wanted to know what was wrong. I told them I was frustrated at the staff because I felt they were being rude.

They said, "We've felt the same way, too, but any time you're frustrated you should just come and talk to us." I felt better because they were there for me to let it out and they didn't make me feel like it was wrong to feel the way I felt.

It wasn't just the girls who were there for me. My therapist, Christie, went out of her way to help. When our sessions were supposed to be an hour, we would talk for two hours because she knew I needed it. She never seemed to judge me, and I always left her office feeling happier.

More and more I found myself opening up and talking about myself and becoming closer to others. After a while I slowly started to accept that I did need others.

EXAMINING MY FEELINGS

Christie helped me understand why I acted the way I did, and with that I was able to understand how I could change. I had to fill out a thought process sheet when I broke the rules, like if I cussed or talked back to the staff. I would have to write what upset me, how I responded, what I could have done differently, and how upset I was on a scale of 1 to 10. I would think, "I can't believe I did that." It was helpful because I got a lot of stuff off my chest. I wasn't holding as much inside.

> **Now I can stop myself from letting my emotions get out of hand and acting on them in the wrong way. If I get angry, I'll feel anger, but I'll also understand it's really frustration because I feel like I'm not being listened to.**

Now I can stop myself from letting my emotions get out of hand and acting on them in the wrong way. If I get angry, I'll feel anger, but I'll also understand it's really frustration because I feel like I'm not being listened to. And instead of yelling, I'll stay calm.

Gradually my behavior started to improve and I followed the rules more often. The better my behavior was, the more privileges I got, like going with the staff and other girls to the movies, mini-golf, and restaurants. When I was finally allowed to leave the facility by myself, I felt proud. I didn't have anywhere to go so I walked to the grocery store and bought my friend Jell-O because I knew she liked it.

DISCUSSING, NOT YELLING

Eventually my therapist, the staff, and my mom felt I was ready to leave Excelsior and live in a place without as many rules. On my last day at Excelsior they threw a going-away party for me with cake and ice cream. I spent the night hanging out with my friends and staff. All of my friends signed a journal, writing good-bye letters saying that they'd miss me and that they hoped I would continue to improve. As good as it was to read those things, what made it better was that I believed what they were saying. I could see the change in myself.

The day before my 15th birthday, I came back to California. I moved into a group home in Los Angeles where I lived with staff and five other girls. The group home was temporary so I could eventually go home to my mom.

I was excited about being at the group home. It wasn't as strict and the staff and the girls were friendly. I joked with the staff that Excelsior dealt with the "bad girl," and they got the "good girl."

I moved back home in September. I hadn't lived at home since I was 11 and now I'm 16. Things are better. I don't yell at my mom anymore. When we disagree, we have discussions. For example, last month my mom and I debated what school I should go to. I wanted to go to a less restrictive school that focused more on my education than on my behavioral issues. I explained to her that I didn't feel like I needed to be in the restrictive school. She told me that her options were limited, but that she would take everything I said into consideration.

I felt good about the conversation because I felt like she was trying her best to understand where I was coming from and I understood where she was coming from. It made me feel more comfortable talking to her and closer to her.

I'm lucky my mom sent me to Excelsior when she did. If I hadn't gotten help, I would be a lot different now. I think I would've ended up running away from home or hanging out with bad people. It has been a struggle getting to be the person I am today. I am a loving, friendly, outgoing girl. I don't think I am anywhere near done growing and learning about who I am, but I have come very far.

EXPLAINING MY LIFE

by Shateek Palmer

The first time I ever wrote about my feelings was when my grandmother was placed in the hospital. I was 9 years old. I knew I had to be strong for her, so I wrote about how much I loved her. I wrote in a notebook because I didn't want to show my feelings to other people.

I felt good when I was writing about my grandmother because I was expressing my feelings without anybody knowing about it. Otherwise I just kept the bad feelings inside, until they came out as anger at someone else.

A week after she went to the hospital, my grandmother died when her liver gave out. After that, all I did was go to school and come home and go to my room. Sometimes I wouldn't eat because I was so hurt. I knew it wasn't healthy how bad I felt.

One night during a thunderstorm, I thought I saw my grandmother in my dark room, and I started to cry. I turned on the light and looked at my notebook and read all the wonderful things I'd written about my grandmother. Then I picked up a pen and wrote like there was no tomorrow.

I wrote about all the negative things that had happened in my life. By the time I was done writing, I realized that my grandmother was in a better place. When I wrote, I felt like I was doing something with my life because I wasn't feeling mad or sad.

But two months later, I found out that ACS (New York City's Children's Services) was taking my three younger siblings and me away from my grandfather and my mother. My mother had always moved in and out of the house and made things stressful for my grandparents and for me. After I was moved to the ACS building, I didn't care about life. I felt even worse than when my grandmother died. I didn't talk to anyone, didn't eat at times, and couldn't sleep. I just stayed in the room that I was placed in.

I had so much anger in me, I started to take it out on people. I got into fights and I didn't respect anybody. I just didn't care about anything.

A BAD SURPRISE

I was placed in a foster home a month later. I remember that night like it was today. The ACS workers put my siblings and me in a dark blue van. I had in my head that I was going back to my grandfather's house.

"I have a surprise for all of you," said one of the ACS staff.

I was really happy because I thought that we were going home. The van took off like it was in a race, but then we stopped in front of a building I didn't know.

"What's going on?" I asked.

"Take the little kids upstairs; I want to talk to Shateek for a moment," said one of the ACS workers.

I felt like this person was about to tell me something disappointing like everybody else had, and you best believe I was right. "Shateek, you can't go back with your family now. We are placing you in a better home for now. I need you to be strong for your siblings and also for yourself. Please behave and listen to these people; they are really good people," the worker said.

I began to cry as we walked out of the van. I was so upset with my family; I felt like I never wanted to talk to them again. We walked into the building and up the stairs to the third floor. The worker showed me my room and said, "Good luck with this family; I'll be back to check up on you."

> **I realized that it's healthier to write your feelings on a piece of paper than to let your emotions affect you in a negative way. But my anger and sadness were so strong that I began to fight again, disobey my foster parents, and do badly in school. I just didn't want to listen to anybody because I felt alone in the world, like I was the only person going through problems.**

That whole night I couldn't sleep. I kept walking around the house. I was thinking about running away, but I didn't want to leave my siblings. So I began to write my feelings. I realized again that it's healthier to write your feelings on a piece of paper than to let your emotions affect you in a negative way.

But my anger and sadness were so strong that I began to fight again, disobey my foster parents, and do badly in school. I just didn't want to listen to anybody because I felt alone in the world, like I was the only person going through problems.

A STACK OF NOTEBOOKS

I stayed with the foster family for about a month and a half. Then I was placed into my great-aunt Stacey's home, where I still live. I was a little happier living with people I knew. Writing also continued to help make me less mad at the world. When I got mad at something or someone, I would walk away. The moment I got home, I would write about it. Like all teenage kids, I did get into a little trouble, but not as much trouble as I got into before.

To this day, I still write in a notebook, usually three pages every night before bed. It takes two to three weeks to fill up a notebook, and I have a stack of notebooks next to my dresser, starting from when I was 10.

I usually start by writing about the day, but often I go back in time to when I was 9 years old. I write about how my grandmother died, how I was taken away from my family, how I messed up in school, and how I got into a lot of fights. I describe the difference between what's going on in my life now and what I went through when I was 9. I wouldn't really talk directly about upsetting things like that when I was 9.

Now I'm 15 and, partly because of writing, I can control my emotions better. When I was younger I didn't understand where all that anger was coming from and why I got in so much trouble. But when I look back at it now I'm like, "Wow, that kid went through a lot!" By writing, I can forgive the 9-year-old Shateek.

COMMUNICATION

I also started to write poetry when I was 10 years old. I don't use stanzas or make my poems rhyme; I just put how I feel about things. Unlike my notebook, I read over my poetry and look for mistakes and things I want to improve.

Here's something from a poem I wrote when I was feeling lonely and didn't have anyone to talk to. It's called "Bad things, good things":

> **"Fight after fight in trouble all the time, I say to myself, What a life, I wish I could bring back time. It's hard dealing with a pain that won't go away, it's like fighting something that's a part of you. I feel tears coming down but I won't let myself cry."**

"Losing a lot doesn't make you a man or a woman, it's just losing something. Anger inside want to release but how should I, in a lost world with no one to listen. Fight after fight in trouble all the time, I say to myself, What a life, I wish I could bring back time. It's hard dealing with a pain that won't go away, it's like fighting something that's a part of you. I feel tears coming down but I won't let myself cry."

Writing really helped me when I started counseling, too. At first, I didn't really speak that much to my counselor, but one day I wanted to show off my writing talent to her. I also wanted to share my feelings with her, but I was afraid that she really didn't care. I felt that she was only there because she was getting paid.

But writing got us communicating (we also played games). Then we started to talk more about how I was feeling and I began to trust her. She introduced me to *Represent*[1]. I guess she noticed something in me that I didn't notice—that my writing was good enough to share with other people in a magazine.

Getting picked for the *Represent* summer writing workshop made me really proud of myself. It took me six years to realize that I had something special in me and that I just had to

---

[1] Represent is a magazine written by and for teens in foster care, published by Youth Communication.

believe in myself. Now I can share my feelings and experiences with other kids who may also be angry about losing their families.

TAMING MY ANGER

by Tray T.

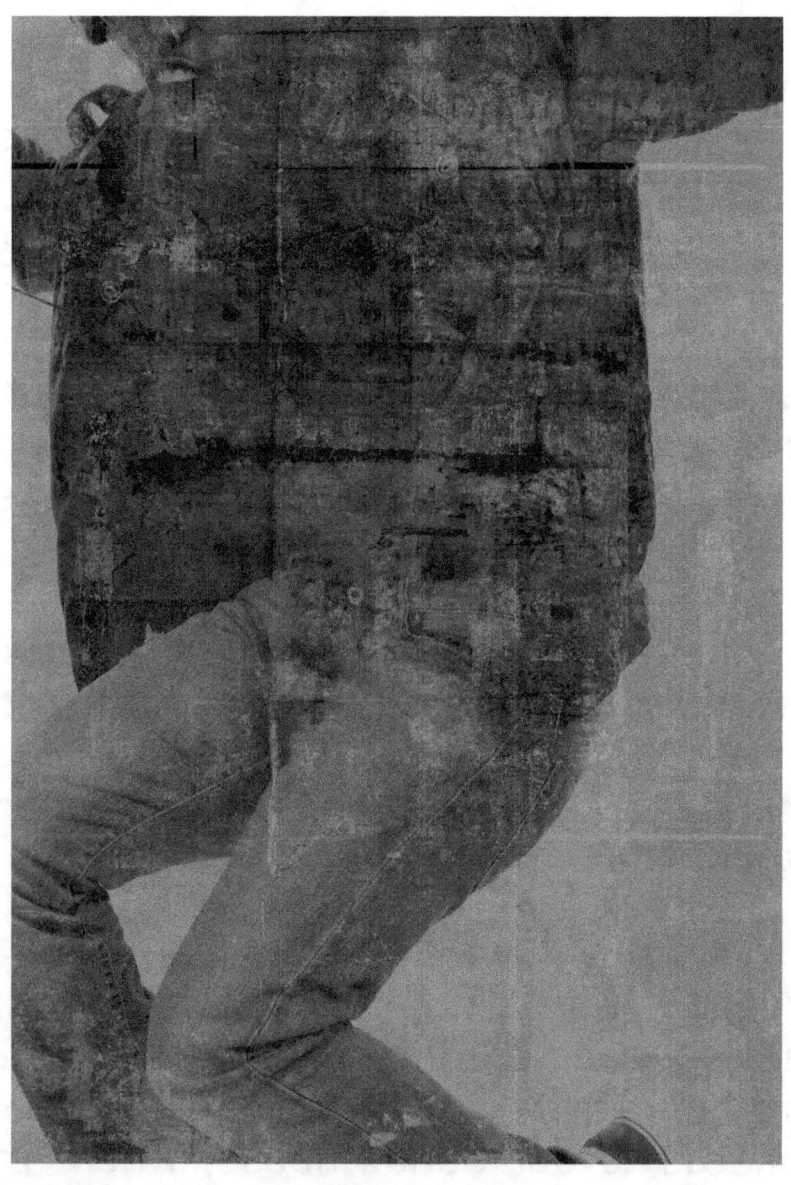

At my group home they called me Cupcakes. They took my things and threw water in my face. Once, when I was asleep, a boy urinated in a cup and threw it on my covers. Another time, a boy set my bed on fire when I wasn't there, then he and four other kids jumped me. I beat them up and trashed their rooms.

Being in foster care is hard. But being gay in foster care takes the struggle to a whole new level. Anger became my weapon against those who antagonized me, but over time I came to realize that my anger also threatened to destroy me.

> **Anger became my weapon against those who antagonized me, but over time I came to realize that my anger also threatened to destroy me.**

My angry ways began long before, when I was a child. My mother did drugs, and she'd leave my younger brother, sister, and me alone. Or she'd take us to our aunt's house, where my older male cousins sexually abused me.

They told me not to tell anyone and that if I did, they would do it again.

For a long time I felt like everyone was out to hurt me. Because of my mom's neglect and the horrible things my cousins did to me, I felt no one loved me. I kept that inside for a long time, until it turned into rage.

When I was 7 I was put in foster care, but that didn't stop my anger. In my first foster home I got into an argument with my foster mom over my long hair. She said that it was feminine. I said I didn't give a damn.

Later that night she came into my room while I was asleep and cut my hair. The next morning when I saw my hair on my pillow, I went off. I got a broom, went to her room, and hit her in her sleep. Then I destroyed her living room. For the next five years, I never lived in one foster home longer than a few months.

When I started living in group homes, I tried hard to keep the other boys from finding out that I was gay. After I beat up the boys who had called me Cupcakes, the staff felt I was in danger so they moved me to another group home. Things didn't get any better.

I got restrained several times a month for fighting. With my temper and weighing almost 300 pounds, it took five or six staff to pin me. But after a while, I started secretly going out with a guy I liked. It got around to the staff, and my therapist told me about GLASS (Gay and Lesbian Adolescent Social Services), a program for gay and lesbian kids in Los Angeles.

I was tired of kids calling me names and trying to fight me because I was gay, so I agreed to go to GLASS. I thought I was going to do well. But I didn't realize I would have to get used to a new environment and new people all over again.

When I first went to GLASS I was the old Tray again. Kids knew not to mess with me when I gave my look—rolling my eyes and raising my lip. The whole room would clear when I was going to get into a fight. The staff would have to pull me off. Sometimes I liked being the person people were scared of. I had control—or so I thought.

Then one day, after I'd been at GLASS about six months, a staff person made me think about things in a new way.

She told us that when she was younger she'd imagined different ways she might end up, like being a prostitute, robbing people, or being homeless. Then she imagined herself working with kids and realized that's what she wanted to do with her life.

It made me imagine my own future. I imagined myself hurting somebody and ending up in jail. I imagined myself on the streets. That made me want to change.

Around the same time, my social worker was getting fed up with me. He told the staff that if anything else happened they should call the police to take me to jail. I was pissed off, but I was also scared. It was time to straighten up.

But it was hard to change because being angry was all I knew how to be. I took baby steps. I went to therapy. I also found someone I could trust.

Her name was Isabelle and she was one of the group home staff. One time

I got in an argument with her. She wouldn't back down. She said, "I can see something in you. I know you can go far and I'm going to help you." I started going to her when something made me angry.

I also started to accept that I was gay. When I arrived at GLASS I didn't know there were young people who were openly gay. It was weird seeing gay people who were acting feminine and flamboyant. I had always known I was gay, but I didn't want to admit it. I realized that GLASS was where I belonged, where I could be open and not be made fun of.

One day I said, "I'm gay." The kids said, "Girl, we already knew." I busted out wearing a rainbow belt.

Being able to be myself made me happier. I made friends. I started listening to the staff's suggestions for ways to keep calm. When I was mad I'd count to 10, dance in my room, or sit in a chair and listen to my stereo, bobbing my head to the music. Or I'd ignore the person and talk to staff or my friends. I signed up for art and dancing groups.

> **It made me imagine my own future. I imagined myself hurting somebody and ending up in jail. I imagined myself on the streets. That made me want to change.**

I still had my ups and downs. One time I went off on a staff person at my group home because she didn't know how to cook. Isabelle overheard and pulled me out of the kitchen. We talked about it. I was getting older and I saw I couldn't do these things anymore.

When I was 15 I moved to another group home at GLASS. I became friends with one of the girls, Tiffany. She was the only person to stand up to me, which made me respect her. We talked about relationships and stuff in our lives, and I knew Tiffany wasn't going to give up on me.

Everything was going real good. Then, on my 16th birthday, I went to my mother's house and my cousin tried to molest me again. I told him I wasn't a child anymore and was big enough and old enough to defend myself, so he backed off.

When I came back I told my therapist. It was the first time I'd told someone about what happened to me. I knew that if I wanted to get somewhere, it had to start now. Talking about it made me less angry.

I was voted president of the Resident Advisory Board, a group that plans fun activities. In June we set up an open mike. Tiffany, me, and another girl in our house did a dance routine to hip-hop and R & B. We laughed and played around as we practiced in the living room, each of us throwing our own moves in. I love dancing because it makes me feel like I'm not vulnerable. It puts me in a place where I'm far away and free.

I sometimes visit my brother and sister, who got adopted. But I have no contact with my mom. It's too much pain.

GLASS is my family now. I feel loved. The staff makes me feel like I always have someone to talk to. I know they expect more out of me. It makes me want to do well because I know I will let them down if I mess up.

I still argue and get upset, but I don't go off. When I see other kids acting like beasts—destroying things, fighting, yelling at staff, and not listening—I see myself. It's a trip because I think, "Damn, I did that."

Some days it still gets me mad that I felt that pain from my cousins, two people who were supposed to love me. But then I think of all the things I went through and I thank God I got through it. I've learned how to deal with my anger in ways that aren't self-destructive, and what I went through is now making me stronger.

***

Tray wrote this story for *LA Youth,* a paper by and for teens. Copyright © *LA Youth.* Reprinted with permission.

THE LIFE AND DEATH OF THE CRIPPLED ENIGMA

by Otis Hampton

I've been angry for as long as I can remember. It started when I was 2 and I was given up for adoption. Foster parents took me in when I was 5 and then adopted me when I was 9. I had grown to love my foster father, and then he died, just as my adoption was going through. After his death, I couldn't remember how to smile anymore.

My foster mother told me that my biological mother gave me up because "you were sick and she couldn't take care of you." I never understood that. Being sick just didn't seem like a good enough reason to give up your son. Every time my foster mother said that—whenever we had "family meetings"—I grew so angry that I would take it out on my younger (adoptive) brother by beating him up, or on my mother by yelling and cursing at her. I would also get angry at anyone who brought up the subject of my birth parents. I got in a lot of fights and broke a lot of objects.

The first things I wrote about were my feelings about the death

> **of my adoptive father and also about being given up by my birth mother. Basically I wrote some form of "I'm angry" over and over. It made me feel like I had a voice.**

My social worker Katie suggested I write about whatever I felt instead of taking out my frustrations on people. So I wrote "Otis's Notebook" on the front of an empty notebook. The first things I wrote about were my feelings about the death of my adoptive father and also about being given up by my birth mother. Basically I wrote some form of "I'm angry" over and over. It made me feel like I had a voice.

But that got repetitive. Fairy tales and other kids' books inspired me to create, and I started making up my own stories. The stories were based on my life and also dreams and fantasies. I would write about whatever happened in school and, if I was in the mood, I would make my character the hero of a battle to win the girl's heart. The characters were me and my friends from school, and the damsel in distress was always Carla.

I fell in love with Carla when I was 6. She was the only one who could keep me calm. She could grab my upraised fist and pull it down and make my anger go away. We were inseparable for a few years.

Writing my stories had a similar effect. I was so caught up in what I was writing about that all my anger just faded away as though it never existed. There were no problems with anyone in the family: no fights, no screaming, no cursing—just peace and quiet. I actually thought that the angry Otis who cursed and yelled was gone. The stories that I wrote only depicted happiness. I wanted the fictions of my stories to mix into the reality of who I was. It was an escape from just being angry all the time.

In junior high, real life pissed me off even more. My friends from sixth grade turned on me in seventh grade. I never understood why, but that's when I learned that the people you call friends can stab you in the back.

In seventh-grade English class, we read classic poems like Edgar Allen Poe's "The Raven." I thought, "Let me give writing my own poem a shot. It's like telling a story." As with my first stories, my poems weren't angry. My first poem was inspired by what I felt the first time I saw Carla. I wrote about her sensitivity, her captivating smile, and the mesmerizing soul that you would only sense if you held her hand.

Carla moved away when I was 13. We continued to talk on the phone, but it was never the same. After I lost her, I didn't feel that there was any hope for me in terms of love.

Around the same time, I was also becoming a teenager, and the tone of my writing and my attitudes changed completely. I couldn't understand what I was doing, why I was cursing at my mother, why I was writing such dark poetry. Though I had loved Carla, I doubted the love that other kids said they felt. In junior high, when Valentine's Day came around, I would sit at the back of the classroom and write poems like this one: "Roses are red, 50 Cent can't rap, Girls smell like perfume, YOU SMELL LIKE CRAP." To amuse myself, I sent those poems out as "gifts" to my friends and sometimes to people who picked on me.

> **"Roses are red, 50 Cent can't rap, Girls smell like perfume, YOU SMELL LIKE CRAP."**

By the time I entered 10th grade, I realized I was on my own. I didn't want anything to do with all the fights and troublemaking I saw. Some of my classmates were already having sex at 15 and talking about wedding plans, for Christ's sake! Others were talking about getting high and being in gangs. I didn't want to be like them, so I retreated into writing about what I saw.

I created a writing persona to describe the doom that would befall the gang members and other evildoers. I called him the Crippled Enigma. The name was inspired in part by the professional wrestler Jeff Hardy, known as the Charismatic Enigma. And I walked with a limp, so the Crippled Enigma was born. I used the name on one of my Myspace pages and for a website called Gspoetry. The Crippled Enigma was a part of me that no one ever got to see before—dark, cynical, theatrical, like Heath Ledger's Joker from *The Dark Knight.* His writing was full of sarcasm, humiliation, and violence.

The poems I wrote as CE channeled my anger at being bullied, losing Carla, not being listened to by my mother, and anything else that upset me. The poems were an outlet that allowed me to express my feelings without revealing anything too personal. Whenever I needed to blow off a little steam, the Crippled Enigma could take on the negative aspects of my life, protecting the weak and innocent version of me. He was all-powerful, without doubt or pity.

And it turned out, people liked the Crippled Enigma. The audience on Gspoetry made me feel like I had a family of poets who always wanted to listen to everything I had to say. Whether I showed my darkness or hid it, I was still appreciated as a poet and as a human being in general. I didn't want to write to impress people, but I did want to be accepted, and I needed an audience.

There was a similar tension in my real life: I wanted to fit in at school without actually having to be like everyone else. I found myself acting like the Crippled Enigma, the writing persona that people online complimented and adored. The Crippled Enigma became a mask that I could hide my real self behind.

The mask was also protection from conflict. If I was jeered by bullies, the Crippled Enigma would taunt them: "Tell me child, do you love yourself and the mind you possess? Or were you neglected and beaten so you decided to take it out on me?" The Crippled Enigma knew how to make them feel bad for picking on me.

The Crippled Enigma could also keep girls and their nosy questions away. One time I was sitting on the bleachers in the gym. A few girls were sitting one level above me. I was listening to my headphones and I didn't notice that one of the girls had come down to sit next to me.

Said the girl: "What are you writing?"

Said I, sarcastically: "It's called a poem ... you know, where sometimes you rhyme."

Said the girl: "You mad mean, I'm not retarded, I know what a poem is."

Said I, sarcastically: "I'm sure you do. With that kind of knowledge, you can shoot for the stars ... and then wake up."

She walked away crying, and I thought, "Oh crap." I didn't want to make anyone feel bad; I just wanted to be left alone. The next day, I saw the girl, but she ran away. Then I handed her a poem entitled "Apology (What I Meant to Say Was...)," which I wrote after I saw her in tears. I wrote the poem because the words "I'm sorry" just didn't come out the way I wanted them to. I was ashamed by the grief that I had caused that poor girl.

I started thinking about making that girl cry and how intimidating I was to some people and it disturbed me. "He's one scary kid," "He's gonna mess you up," "Leave him alone"—these were phrases I kept hearing as I walked the halls and I thought, "This isn't me. Otis doesn't hurt anyone's feelings, Otis doesn't scare people." The Crippled Enigma and his anger had taken over too much of my life. Some mornings, I'd wake up pissed off and look in the mirror and it wouldn't be Otis staring back. It'd be the Crippled Enigma—the storm that killed the calm as opposed to the calm that killed the storm.

One night not long ago I dreamed about the death of Crippled Enigma. In this dream, I stood at an open grave with an empty casket. Thunder rolled and lightning flashed. Lying there was a body that looked like me but was the Crippled Enigma. I had to hit him in the head with the shovel a few times because he kept waking up, but I stilled him with one final blow and stuffed him in the casket.

What was lying in that casket was in part the pain that had followed me since my birth. The angry, sarcastic, conniving side of me that I used to hurt a person's feelings was the role that the Crippled Enigma had been born to play.

In the dream, the casket went back down six feet under. It felt like shame was being buried. Anger out of control isn't empowering; it's the opposite. My anger is generally over things I couldn't control: being given up for adoption, my dad's death, having cerebral palsy, being bullied. It was worse in a way to have something inside me I couldn't control. The consequences I've faced from letting out all my anger at family, friends, and other innocent people left me feeling ashamed and humiliated.

The dream was a wake-up call for me because it made me realize that I've been using anger as an excuse to upset my family, hurt the feelings of friends, and screw up in life. It made me want to change my ways and think before getting angry and doing something I'd regret for the rest of my life.

But obviously, the anger that has haunted me since childhood isn't gone. Where will it go without the Crippled Enigma to hold it? This is neither the end of my poetry nor my appearances on Gspoetry. But I'd like to be able to keep my anger on the page and out of my life as much as I can.

One way to keep it out of real life is by communicating face-to-face using direct dialogue, without personas. I'd like to get better at ignoring negative influences and at acknowledging people who show me affection.

As far as the page, writing can help me maintain the balance between my anger and my happiness if I don't let the anger take over. A lot of what I see around me is negative, but I can write about it with a lighter and more comfortable voice and with a sense of love and truth to light the darkness. Some of my writing aims to inspire my readers to be themselves instead of everyone else ("Your voice is your weapon, use it with caution/Be careful with the method in every precaution"), or prevent someone from causing harm to himself or others ("Don't fight the enemy, he isn't worth your time/Think about the result before you cross that line"). That's Otis from the heart and from his whole soul.

A lot of what I see around me is negative, but I can write about it with a lighter and more comfortable voice and with a sense of love and truth to light the darkness.

162
READY TO FIGHT

by Joseph Ballew

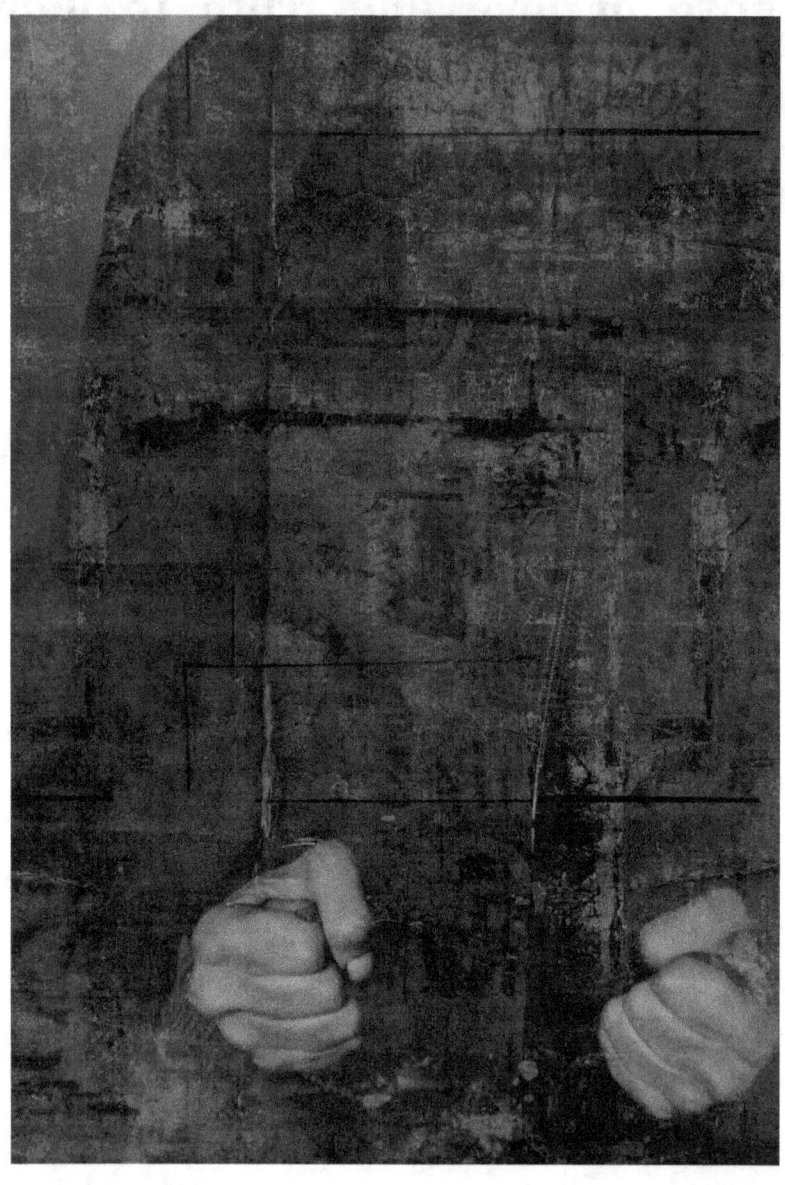

When I moved into my first foster home, I knew it wouldn't be easy. I missed my parents and it's always hard adjusting to strangers. I just hoped that life with my foster mother Linda, her husband Andrew, and their son Tommy, might not be too bad.

At the time, I was very scared. I was only 9 and I didn't even know why I couldn't live with my parents anymore. Not understanding why we were separated made me feel nervous and sad.

The day I met my foster parents, they seemed okay. We went out to restaurants for every meal and played mini-golf. Still, I did not want to live with strangers who I didn't know at all and who knew nothing about me, not even what I liked or didn't like to eat. Going to their home felt like being reborn.

Andrew was calm. He was a police officer and joked with me. We boxed together, watched baseball, basketball, and boxing, and had a lot in common.

But Linda was always angry and yelling. She blamed me for things I did not do and screamed at me for little things, like "Why are your clothes on the bedroom floor?" instead of asking me to pick them up. Whenever Linda had a bad day or was tired, it seemed she took her frustrations out on me.

Linda also hurt my feelings by bringing up my parents when we got in arguments. She called them "alcoholics" and "drug addicts," and said, "They don't know how to take care of their children." She knew I loved my parents and her comments made me angry.

I think we fought so much because the rules and expectations in their home were different from what I'd gotten used to with my parents. My parents never really punished me if I got into trouble in school, and I didn't have to cook, clean, dust, mop, sweep, go to the store, and the whole nine. But my foster parents expected all that, and if I messed up, Linda yelled at me, which I wasn't used to either.

I wished my foster parents would've gone easy on me at first. After all, I was not used to living without my parents, and I was often sad. Instead of trying to understand what I was going through and help me out, the pressure to conform to their family just made it worse.

A couple of months after I moved there, I told my social worker that I did not want to stay there anymore. She told me it might take a month or so for her to find me a new home, and I thought, "Okay."

But that night when I got back home Linda refused to serve me food when everyone else was eating. "You don't live in my house anymore so I am not feeding you," she said.

Later I tried to hop in my bed to go to sleep. Linda said, "Why are you getting in a bed that I paid for?"

"This is the bed that you gave me to sleep in."

"But you're not going to be living here anymore," she said.

I waited about an hour and then begged her to let me sleep in my bed. Finally, she said yes.

I did not tell my social worker or my therapist that Linda tried to punish me for wanting to move, and about a week later I told them that life at Linda's was better, even though it was worse. I lied because the agency still had not found me a new home and I was afraid Linda would get meaner.

> **Living in that home gave me a lot of anger, and my anger changed me. I got so used to being treated badly that I felt like fighting and arguing all the time.**

I was also nervous that the next place I went could be worse. Linda told me that if I left her house, the agency would put me in a group home, and I feared that because I'd heard about kids in group homes fighting and stealing your stuff. So I stayed.

Living in that home gave me a lot of anger, and my anger changed me. I got so used to being treated badly that I felt like fighting and arguing all the time. My education was affected, because all my anger built up in my body and I would take it out on kids and teachers in school.

Soon I wasn't following the rules at home or at school. I was disrespecting authority because I knew Linda didn't care about me when she made the rules, and I didn't think my teachers did, either. When we met with the social worker, Linda put everything on my back, saying I was disrespectful, rude, nasty, and persistent to win a battle. I can't lie. Sometimes I was.

To cope with my anger I would play basketball or baseball, or box with my friends. My friends were fun and made me laugh whenever I was angry or sad. On rainy days, I went to their houses and we watched movies and freestyled.

But the longer I stayed at Linda's, the more I was cut off from my friends and everyone I loved. Linda punished me by telling me I couldn't hang out with my friends. When my family called, she would tell them, "He is not home" when I was. She told my brother not to call her house.

That made me really angry. I would get four quarters and go to a pay phone just to talk to them. Using my own money to call my family when there was a phone in the house made me mad, too.

I felt trapped and imprisoned. I wanted to run away but decided not to because then I would not be able to finish school and wouldn't have a future. Since junior high school, I've been 100 percent sure I am going to college. By staying in care, I could get help paying for college and eventually have a good career. Even during my worst times at Linda's, I stayed on the honor roll.

Then, three months after I turned 16, Linda put me out of the house herself. That day, Linda punished me for talking in my science class and said I couldn't go outside. I started playing a handheld video game, but she snatched it away. We argued.

I said to myself, "I cannot take this anymore" and walked out.

An hour later I came back to find four police cars and an ambulance at my house. The place looked like a murder scene. The ambulance people were there to see if I was psycho, and Linda was telling them I was out of control. After my foster father flipped his badge to the cops to show them he was one, too, I knew no one would listen to me.

I went to a different foster home that night. I had stayed with the foster mother, a lady named Ms. Daniels, once before when Linda went to a family reunion I wasn't invited to. During that time, I had really liked her.

Ms. Daniels had told me she only takes in younger kids, so I thought I'd be moving on. But after a week she told me, "You don't seem like a bad kid, so I'll keep you."

I was really happy. Ms. Daniels let me listen to rap and put up posters of my favorite hip-hop artists in my room. She also let me talk to and see my family whenever I wanted. Ms. Daniels didn't lie to me, go through my things, or say mean things about my parents.

When Ms. Daniels took me with her on vacation to North Carolina to meet her family, a lady pointed to me and asked Ms. Daniels, "Who is that?"

"He's one of my kids," Ms. Daniels said.

I felt really happy when Ms. Daniels said that. Linda always called me her "foster son."

But Ms. Daniels and I have arguments, too, and that worries me. Some of Ms. Daniels's rules are hard for me to follow, like bedtime and curfew. She wants me home by 7p.m.

and in bed by 10:30p.m. Those times are way too early for a 16-year-old! I try to follow her rules, but sometimes I don't, which gets her angry.

Other times I'm sneaky about breaking the rules. If Ms. Daniels tells me, "Go to bed," I'll ask, "Can I finish watching this baseball game and go to bed in 15 minutes?"

The times when she says "No" I will be really angry but try not to show it. I go to my room and watch the game on my own, smaller TV with the volume on really low. One night, she caught me. She just walked over, pressed the "off" button on the TV, and walked out.

Then, a few nights ago, Ms. Daniels told me to get off the phone. When I didn't, she unplugged the jack from the wall. I walked out to finish my conversation with my mother, who lives around the corner, and didn't come back until 10p.m. Ms. Daniels was mad and told me I couldn't use the phone for two weeks.

I don't want our relationship to get bad, and it seems like it is starting to a little bit. I want to listen to her and respect her, but I'm not sure I know how. I got so used to fighting that now I am having a hard time not fighting and arguing.

I know Ms. Daniels is different from Linda, but I don't know how to act differently than I did at Linda's, where I felt like I was fighting an enemy.

Now that I see how much it's affected me to build up my anger in that home, I wish I had spoken up earlier. I wish I'd realized that a good home was waiting just around the corner, and I was wasting time and developing bad habits in the five years I spent with Linda.

I also wish my social worker had kept it confidential when I spoke up, or that she had been able to take me out of the home as soon as I told her there was a problem. I wish she had asked me in confidence if I was still having problems there. Even though I changed my story to protect myself, I think she should've seen that Linda and I were not getting along at all.

I want to stay with Ms. Daniels because I feel she respects me, and this makes me want to try to learn how to respect her. I'm trying to learn a new way of dealing with a foster parent, and to remember that she's not making rules to hurt me. I'm talking to my therapist and social worker about my problems keeping to her rules so this home can work out.

Even my therapist told me, "You look much happier now."

I told her, "I am."

RELEASING MY RAGE

by Miguel Ayala

I've had an anger problem for a long time. It has included crying, yelling, cursing, screaming, and intimidating people. When I was at my worst, I would turn violent and destroy property and throw things. I even tried to kill myself.

The reason I have an anger problem is plain and simple. I grew up in a violent home. My mother would slap, whip, and beat me and my siblings. Also, she would torment us with words that to this day still hurt me. She would call us terrible names if one of us dyed our hair or for messing up on paperwork she was supposed to do. She would beat us for the smallest things, like making noise, or playing too rough in the house, or accidentally breaking things. She'd beat us until we bled or had welts all over our bodies.

> **The reason I have an anger problem is plain and simple. I grew up in a violent home.**

That wasn't the only side of her. Sometimes she would laugh with us, take us on family outings, nurture us, and really show a mother's love. Those times, I really loved her. All this love and hate mixed together made me very confused and angry. Sometimes I took the anger out on myself, sometimes on other people.

When I was 12 my mother gave me $7.50 for a class trip, and instead I bought a video game magazine. She found out and whipped me with an extension cord.

That night I felt so much anger, I didn't know what to do with it. So I contemplated two horrible things. I thought of sneaking out of the apartment, going to my roof, saying a prayer, and then jumping off. And I contemplated hurting my mother. I imagined getting a knife, tiptoeing into my mother's bedroom, and killing her.

In the end, I made it through that night without hurting myself or her. But the worst of my anger was yet to come.

Back then, I never released my rage on my mother. I was afraid that if I did, she might kill me or beat me to the point where I'd be disabled. So instead, I took my rage out on other people, usually at school. I would fight and steal. Many times I would curse at people in public and say obscene things to females. I was a terrible bully.

It made me feel a little better to do those things. It made me feel like I had all the guts in the world, and it released my rage to make other people as mad as I felt. The only problem was that those people would always want to whip my butt for it. Sometimes they did.

Then one day I really lost it. It was a beautiful, warm day. I was 14 or 15. I lost a CD. At first that didn't bother me. Then I started imagining that my mother and brother had taken it just to see me get mad. Thinking this made me angry. I started yelling at my brother and my mom. Then I really went crazy. I was crying, and before I knew it, I'd gone to the china cabinet in the kitchen and rammed my elbow into the glass cover. I cut myself pretty bad. That's when my family sent me to the hospital.

The doctor who bandaged my cut asked me a bunch of questions to see why I did it. But I brushed them off, and said I just lost my temper. They thought of sending me to a residential treatment center where I could get help with my anger, but my mother wouldn't sign the papers to let me go. Looking back, it might have been a good thing for me to go to a residential treatment center where I would have been away from home and might have gotten a lot of adult attention and more mental health services. Instead, I kept living with abuse and feeling angry.

I did go to a school in a hospital because of my behavior problems. There I had therapy and group meetings three times a week for almost two years. They were trying to get me to work on my problems: fights, acting out, acting on impulse, and, my personal favorite, self-destructive behaviors, like when I tried to sharpen my finger in a metal pencil sharpener.

The school was good for me because it gave me a support network of adults who cared. I had all these people who wanted to help me with my problems. It felt like winning the lottery.

Eventually I began to open up to those people. I told one of them that I was contemplating suicide. Telling someone that made me feel a little less alone. But when I started talking with a psychiatrist, I realized I could lose my regular life and go into foster care if I kept telling my secrets, so I tried to just think happy thoughts and act like I didn't have any real problems.

But my anger and thoughts of suicide didn't go away.

One day my brother was cursing a girl on the street, and I thought he was cursing me. So when he came upstairs, I started to curse him out. My mom started to yell at me and sent me to my room. I went to my room and slammed the door. My mom came in my room with a golf club and started to beat me with it. I lost my marbles. I started to yell, curse, and have a tantrum, so the police were called. They thought I was suicidal, so they brought me to the emergency room. Then my mom said, "I don't want him no more." So I was placed in my first group home.

It was a good idea for me to be removed from my mother, but I hated being in a group home. (Still do.) I was so scared and pissed at the same time.

But I also hoped that finally I might get help with my anger problem. It was always getting me into fights and sometimes getting me beaten up. Instead, my anger seemed to get worse.

There were so many things in group-home life that triggered my anger—the bickering, the teasing, the stealing, and the fighting. When I would get into a problem with a resident and staff would intervene, I would curse and stuff like that. Then, when I really needed help from staff, the words I'd said earlier would backfire and the staff wouldn't help me. I got moved to a lot of different group homes because of my anger.

After a while, I started thinking about suicide again. I just couldn't find a way out of my sadness, and I did not trust anyone there enough to talk about my feelings with them. The sadness, was not just connected with my abuse. It was also because of life in the group home. I didn't feel very safe there.

I took out my frustration on myself. I took a knife and slit my

> throat. When I felt no pain, I broke a picture, took a jagged piece of glass from it, and cut my throat again. Soon, I was in the hospital.

I even had a plan: I would either jump off the roof of my mother's building or jump in front of a subway. Then one day I made a spontaneous attempt on my life instead. It was April Fool's Day. That day, a lot of things had gone wrong. My favorite staff member was arrested due to a false allegation. I got into a fight with a friend of mine and he and his brother jumped me. I took out my frustration on myself. In the group home, with people watching, I took a knife and slit my throat. When I felt no pain, I broke a picture, took a jagged piece of glass from it, and cut my throat again.

Soon I was in the hospital. I thought I would be in there forever because of what I'd done to myself.

While I was there, I began to think about a lot of different things that had happened to me. I thought about all the abuse I'd endured in my home and at all the group homes I'd ever lived. It wasn't the pain that bothered me, it was the fact that I would always find myself in the same situation over and over again. It seemed that people were always hitting me—my mom, my foster peers, sometimes even group home staff. I wondered if this pattern would ever stop. What if I got married? Would I face abuse from my spouse? Would I be abused by my kids? Could I break the cycle and try not to be around people who would abuse me? Did I and my anger cause people to abuse me?

There was one patient in the hospital who was old and he couldn't talk or defend himself. He could only grunt. I didn't want to be like him. I didn't want to have the same old problems forever and end up defenseless in a hospital.

> **While I was there, I began to think about a lot of different things that had happened to me. I thought about all the abuse I'd endured in my home and at all the group homes I'd ever lived.**

So I said to myself, "I don't care what it takes. I am going to succeed. I am going to prove to all those who hurt me in my life that I have a future!" I thought maybe I'd want to try to help other people like myself so they would not suffer what I've suffered. To do that, I needed to live.

After my discharge from the hospital, I was motivated to change my life. I started to go back to school. I did my chores and cleaned my room and showed a decent amount of respect to the staff. I started yet another program for my anger. This one paired me with a therapist who was on call 24/7.

Not all those changes stuck. I stopped going to the program after about a month. I don't always do my chores anymore, and I still get in fights. I still struggle with my anger and sometimes when I think about my past, I just want to die. My anger still gets me moved around a lot, and recently I've been running away pretty frequently. But I do feel a little more motivated not to really slip up since I tried to kill myself. I guess that showed me how serious my anger is, and I feel determined not to let that happen again.

Still, I don't know what needs to happen for me to get a firm grip on my anger and emotions. I've been in a lot of programs, and not all of them have had much of an influence on me or my anger. I think the ones that helped the most were the ones where I had a good relationship with the staff there.

I guess my anger problem is the kind of thing that takes a long time to deal with. For now, I try to focus on the positives in my life, and I try not to think about my problems too much. When that doesn't work, I tell myself that if I give in to the stupidity and really lose it, then I'm letting the bullies win.

TEMPER TAMERS?

by Miguel Ayala

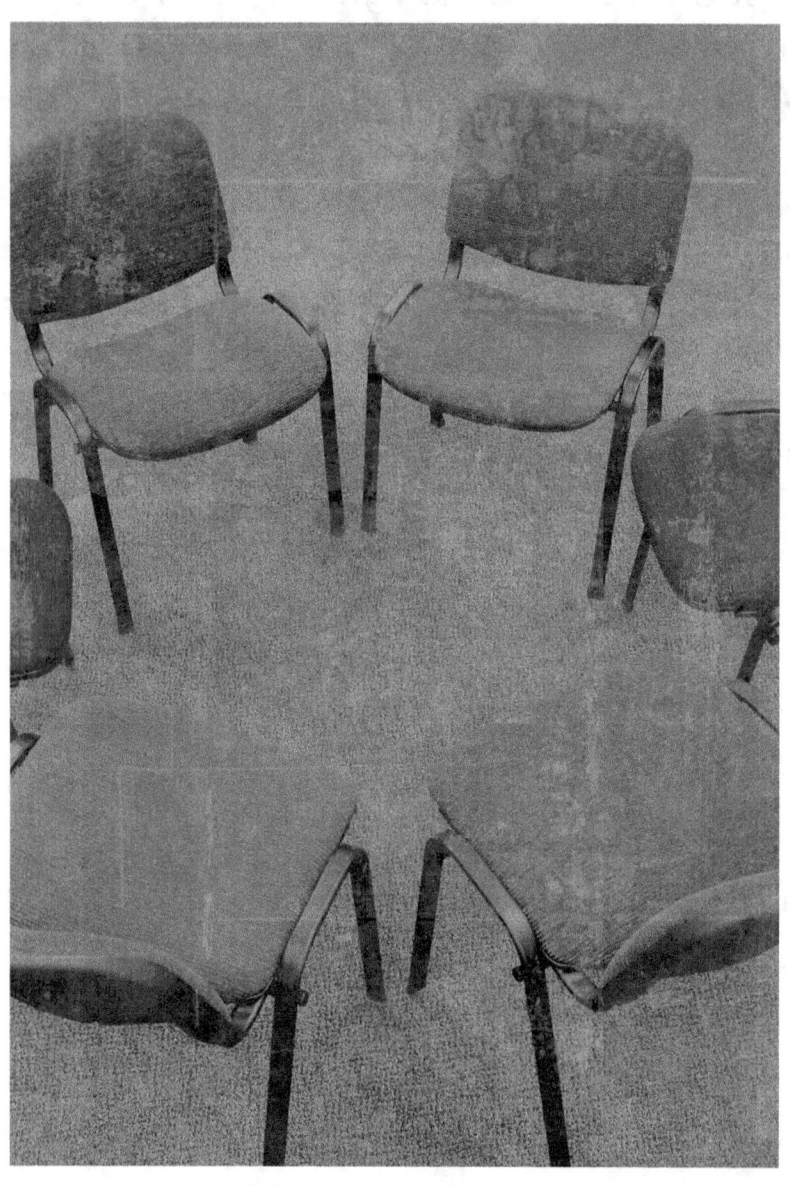

To try to deal with my anger problem, I've been in more programs than you can imagine—programs in hospitals, schools, and community centers. So I have some idea of what works and what doesn't when it comes to trying to help kids get a grip on their lives. Here's a little information about the programs I've been in and what I found useful and useless in them.

When I was in my very first program, I was still living with my mother, who was very abusive. I was 8 years old. The program was located near my mother's house, which was convenient. It provided therapy for children with emotional problems.

I only went four or five times to that program because my mother stopped taking me. I never felt comfortable there, maybe because I didn't go for very long. I didn't like talking about my problems with a person I did not know (the counselor). So I lied to her and told her that I was safe and happy at home.

It made me feel bad to lie, but I was petrified of my mother and I also loved her. I didn't want to tell an outsider about how she hurt me. I thought it would hurt her if I left her care.

After my mom stopped bringing me there, I would've liked it if the counselor kept calling my house and asking why my mom wouldn't bring me there anymore. It would have made me see that she had actually cared, and maybe it would have helped me open up and realize that there is a better world than the one I lived in at that moment. But I was only 8 years old and when I stopped going, I just thought, "Blah!"

My second program was in my junior high school. I met with a counselor twice a week. The counselor let us play music during my sessions and we could do almost anything I wanted. In some sessions, my twin brother Juan would come with me.

At the time, things were flaming between my mother and me. On our 12th birthday, I saw my mother force my brother to take off his clothing and receive 12 lashings—one for each year of our lives—for buying the wrong thing at the store.

> **My beef was that the school was in a double-door locked unit and it was dirty and smelled like a morgue. I felt like I was in jail there, like I was a prisoner of a war, but a war I fought with my own personal demons.**

But again, I didn't trust the counselor enough to say what was inside of me and what was going on at home. Maybe just living at home made it too hard to be open.

My third program was at a hospital that has a school for teens who suffer from emotional problems. Basically, we were going to school on-site with children in the mental health ward.

My beef was that the school was in a double-door locked unit and it was dirty and smelled like a morgue. I felt like I was in jail there, like I was a prisoner of a war, but a war I fought with my own personal demons.

I think it's important for programs to be in friendlier-looking places than that. How do you open up and get help when you feel that uncomfortable?

Still, I think that program helped because it made me see there were other children like me, other children or teens in the city who were also mentally ill. That made me feel more normal and less alone.

My next program helped me a lot. It was in a high school. We had more freedom than at the hospital school, and I formed real relationships with the faculty there. Those relationships made a huge difference in my life. They made me want to be one of the cool kids, one of the students who wouldn't snap or lose control all the time.

The faculty showed me that they really did care. Also, we could leave the school to buy lunch or smoke. That made me feel like they trusted me, and the freedom made me feel happier. We did fun things, like go to a fright event at an amusement park. They also had a prom for us, and took us to college fairs. We even had a student council and a student of the year.

After leaving that school, though, my behavior was bad. Now I was trying to fight back, intimidating and manipulating my mother.

The next program provided family services and mental health services. After liking the last program so much, I knew that the people were also trying to help me, and I received them with open arms.

I liked the staff there. I had a lot of fun with my staff worker, Joe Hunt. He was cool and he would tell jokes and make me feel good about myself. It was the best program I was ever in because I built a relationship with Joe based on trust and honesty where there were no phony smiles. He and the other staff actually cared, and that was the right thing they could do. They were the ones who helped get me into foster care.

> **Looking back on all the programs I've been in, it seems that what helped me most was when the staff really cared about me and I could build a relationship with them.**

Looking back on all the programs I've been in, it seems that what helped me most was when the staff really cared about me and I could build a relationship with them. It's also helpful to do fun things in a friendly, spacious environment to help everyone feel comfortable, and to be with other kids who have similar problems, to help kids with problems feel less alone. And I think it's better to have freedom than a too-restrictive setting.

Freedom helped me feel more responsible and trusted. But I think it was hard for me to really focus on my problems while I was still living with my mother. For me to get better while I was living with her, she would have had to get better, too.

CHANGING THE PATTERN

by Anonymous

It's a weekday evening. I'm sitting on top of my bed, sobbing profusely. I just received a beating from Mother. What did I do to deserve it? I can't really remember.

Sometimes I'd get beat if I talked back to Grandma. Other times, for touching something in the house that didn't belong to me. Or for forgetting to clean out the tub after I'd used it. It really didn't matter what I'd get beaten for. At the end of some whippings, I'd sit on my bed and say to myself, "When I have kids, I'm never gonna beat them."

> **Mother thought children were victims of abuse only if they were sexually molested, beaten into unconsciousness, or abandoned in the streets. No, to Mother I wasn't being abused. She was simply raising me the best way she knew how.**

Mother demanded that I take my punishment in dignity and silence, "like a woman," she would sneer. Any yelping or whimpering from me would cause her to strike again. Beatings were endless, until I choked, literally, to hold down the screams.

You will read this, I'm sure, and conclude that I was a victim of abuse. But at the time, it wasn't obvious to either Mother or me. You see, Mother thought children were victims of abuse only if they were sexually molested, beaten into unconsciousness, or abandoned in the streets.

No, to Mother I wasn't being abused. She was simply raising me the best way she knew how.

During my first year in foster care, after tearful nights and weekly sessions with the resident therapist, I was able to acknowledge to myself that I had been abused. However, I wasn't aware that Mother's abusive patterns were very much alive and growing within me.

In the group home I was known for my hot temper and quick, violent ways of ending disputes. Little mistakes made by the girls would send me flying into a hot rage. I'd cool off only after several doors had been kicked and a few glasses broken. Concerned counselors would pull me aside, but I waved away my actions as just "blowing off steam."

Last year I visited my grandmother's house one weekend. (My mother, my aunt Lunette, and my cousin Clyde also lived there.) On this particular weekend, both Auntie Lunette and Mother were at work. Grandmother and Clyde were home. After about an hour of chatting and watching television, Grandma stepped away to take a shower, leaving me to tend to young Clyde.

Before leaving, she gave me specific instructions to call for her if Clyde misbehaved. "Don't give your cousin any trouble, Clyde," she said and went off. Well, as soon as Clyde heard water running in the shower, he decided to turn the television from the Thanksgiving parade to the cartoon channel, which Grandma had advised him not to do.

"Yo, Clyde," I said sternly, "chill with the TV."

In minutes, a matter as trivial as what TV station to watch evolved into a major dispute, which Clyde ended with the words, "You're not my mother. I'm not listening to you."

I felt humiliated. Here I was, 18 years old, being dictated to by someone eight years my junior. I wanted Clyde to listen. I wanted him to obey me. So I did to him what Mother had done to me so many times before. I hit him across the face with the back of my hand.

> **I did to him what Mother had done to me so many times before. I hit him across the face with the back of my hand.**

In doing so, I was careful not to cause him too much pain, but enough to make him realize I was serious. He shouted in agony and rushed my legs with punches as hard as his little hands could throw.

"What?!?" I said, both shocked and angry that this 10-year-old had actually hit me back. In a moment, faster than it takes for a person to think, I grabbed the remote control and swung it at Clyde's head. Everything happened so quickly. The remote dropped from my hand and my body trembled as I noticed blood streaming from a gash in Clyde's forehead.

"Oh my God oh my God oh my God, I didn't mean to hit you, Clyde!"

He was screaming at the top of his lungs. Never had I seen so much blood. I tried to subdue his screams and put my hands over his mouth, but Clyde shoved me away and yelled all the louder.

At this point, I was more worried about stopping the blood than keeping him quiet. Wads of red Kleenex tissue were strewn on the floor. In looking at the amount of blood this kid was shedding, I panicked. Clyde might need medical attention. Grandma heard the screams and came running out of the shower, wet and dripping, clad only in a towel.

"Oh my gosh! I leave you with Clyde for one minute and this is what happens?" she cried. She pulled him into the bathroom and was able to stop the bleeding. I walked back into Grandma's room, stared out the window, blankly reflecting on what had taken place in a matter of seconds. "My temper," I said to myself. "I need help."

Minutes later Grandma came back, freshly clothed, along with Clyde. His face and neck were wiped clean of blood. There was nothing but a small bandage, smack dab across the center of his forehead.

I could only stand there and look at him. I had wanted him to be afraid of me just so he would obey. And now I had left a scar on him. Grandma split the blame between us—Clyde for not listening and me for hitting him. But there was nothing she could say to rid me of my guilt. At first, I was going to hang around until Mother got home from work, but now I decided it wouldn't be such a good idea.

The train ride from Brooklyn to my group home in lower Manhattan was agonizing. I listened to music in an attempt to forget what happened, but there was no distracting me. Echoes of Clyde's frightful screams filled my brain. I spread the palms of my hands and stared at them for a while, not quite believing that I had hurt a child, my own cousin no less.

A couple of minutes prior to entering my group home, I looked at my reflection in a car window and checked for any traces of tears. "I'm fine," I assured myself, choked up though I was. I walked onto my floor and the area was bustling with activity, as is normal on a Saturday afternoon.

Before I could even duck and hide myself in my room, one of the girls called out, "Hey, you got blood on your shirt."

That did it. The protective wall I'd built for myself was crumbling fast, and I needed to talk. Barbara, the staff on duty at the time, pulled me to the patio where it was more private. Five cigarettes later, I spilled the beans. I told her everything—how I felt, what I did, and how sincerely sorry I was.

Barbara sympathized with me, but did agree that I was in need of help, professional or otherwise. She also pointed out that my violent tendencies may have stemmed from the abuse I experienced as a child. As I mentioned before, I did accept having been abused by my mother. But until now, I hadn't accepted or even dealt with being a potential abuser of others.

It was somewhat disturbing to think that I was becoming exactly what I hated in my mother. Part of me wanted to remain in the comfort of denial, but I knew that minimizing the seriousness of the situation would lead to more expressions of violence.

One helpful outlet for me was the self-help book *Anxiety, Phobias, & Panic: Taking Charge and Conquering Fear* by Reneau Z. Peurifoy. It was comforting to see that someone had taken the time to write out what I had experienced and what I was feeling.

> **It was somewhat disturbing to think that I was becoming exactly what I hated in my mother. Part of me wanted to remain in the comfort of denial, but I knew that minimizing the seriousness of the situation would lead to more expressions of violence.**

For example, in the first chapter, "What, Why, and How," Peurifoy talks about the general anxieties people suffer from and how they are linked to the abuse they experienced as children. I was shocked to find that I possessed many of the traits that characterize someone as having high anxiety—namely, the excessive need for approval, extremely high expectations of oneself, and an excessive need to be in control.

But the scariest was yet to be found. In the following paragraphs, there was a list of family factors that led to a person having such a "high-anxiety" personality. I suffered from all the factors, including alcoholism in the family and a rigid belief system (meaning that your parents set up strict rules for everything, without room for compromise). It was upsetting to see that I experienced more than one "high-anxiety" factor in my family. Most people have a hard time swallowing this kind of information.

While reading this book, I continued to see Ms. Hoffman, the therapist assigned to me at the group home. She was helpful for a time, but I needed to do more than talk about the problem and discuss the possible solutions. I had to apply these solutions to my life and practice them daily.

For example, during the last three weeks of school I had to put in a lot of study time. That meant either staying at the Chelsea Library until closing time or locking myself in my room. I preferred to stay home and study. The problem was, I shared my space with two other girls. So every five minutes or so, I had to get up from my desk to open the door for them, which eventually got annoying.

Rather than telling them to go to hell, I left the door open just a crack to avoid getting up. All was quiet on the Western front until the girls turned up the volume on the television to watch *The Muppet Show.*

At this point I could've dealt with this situation as I did with Clyde when I didn't get my way: by yelling at or even hitting the girls. And again, as with Clyde, I was experiencing an "excessive need to be in control." But unlike the incident with Clyde, I understood why I was angry. So I shoved down the temptation and instead shut the door that sectioned off the hallway from the living room and things quieted down.

In dealing with anger, it is wise not to put yourself in situations that will upset you. I had to admit that if I had turned in my school assignments on time, I wouldn't have had to rush at the last minute and be an inconvenience to everyone. I had to acknowledge that I had responsibility for my anger.

Another productive outlet was journal writing. I didn't write entries at the end of the day as some might do, but during those times when the thought of shoving my fist down someone's throat was most tempting. In a month's time, not only was I able to analyze my feelings and pinpoint exactly what things would trigger my fits of anger, but I sharpened my skills as a writer as well.

Even though I have made a sincere effort to curb my anger, it still comes out every now and then. One incident happened last summer when I entered a relationship with a sister (let's call her Lydia). Even before getting serious about this particular woman, I never thought there would come a time when I'd want to hurt her intentionally if she did something to aggravate me. Well, lo and behold.

It was a Saturday morning at her apartment and I was downstairs by the washing machine sorting out our clothes. There was no one there but me.

Someone yelled my name and I jumped out of my skin. I turned around and Lydia was staring at me with a box of detergent in her hands. It wasn't her intention to frighten me. She had come to tell me that I had forgotten the fabric softener.

> **In dealing with anger, it is wise not to put yourself in situations that will upset you.**

Well, I just didn't see it that way at the time. I was so angry that I raised a bottle and smashed it on the dryer. It was as if I'd been possessed. Once again, I was scared of my reaction. I walked to the window and took a few deep breaths. I turned around to apologize to Lydia and she was gone. "I'm sorry," I said to the space where she once stood. "I'm sorry."

I went back to the apartment and she looked at me like I was a total stranger. A few days after the incident, Lydia approached me with great concern. She feared that the next time I exploded, I would do worse—perhaps hit her.

I apologized and assured Lydia that I could never lay a finger on her in malice. But deep down I realized that just as I had not intended to hit Clyde with the remote control months earlier, it had happened. I wasn't too sure that it wouldn't happen again, but I felt I had a better chance of dealing with it.

Of course, as with the other situations, there were alternatives to smashing that bottle against the dryer. One is using breathing techniques, one of the many methods Dr. Peurifoy lists at the end of each chapter that have really helped me in dealing with my anger and phobias. By the end of Chapter 2, I had learned several methods of breathing that are very effective in calming me in stressful situations.

> **No matter what form of help you seek in dealing with anger, none will guarantee you an overnight solution. It's like writing with your left hand your whole life and suddenly deciding to switch to your right.**

No matter what form of help you seek in dealing with anger, none will guarantee you an overnight solution. It's like writing with your left hand your whole life and suddenly deciding to switch to your right.

I still get angry. But there is relief in knowing that I'm doing something about it.

ANGER THAT WON'T LET GO

by Natasha Santos

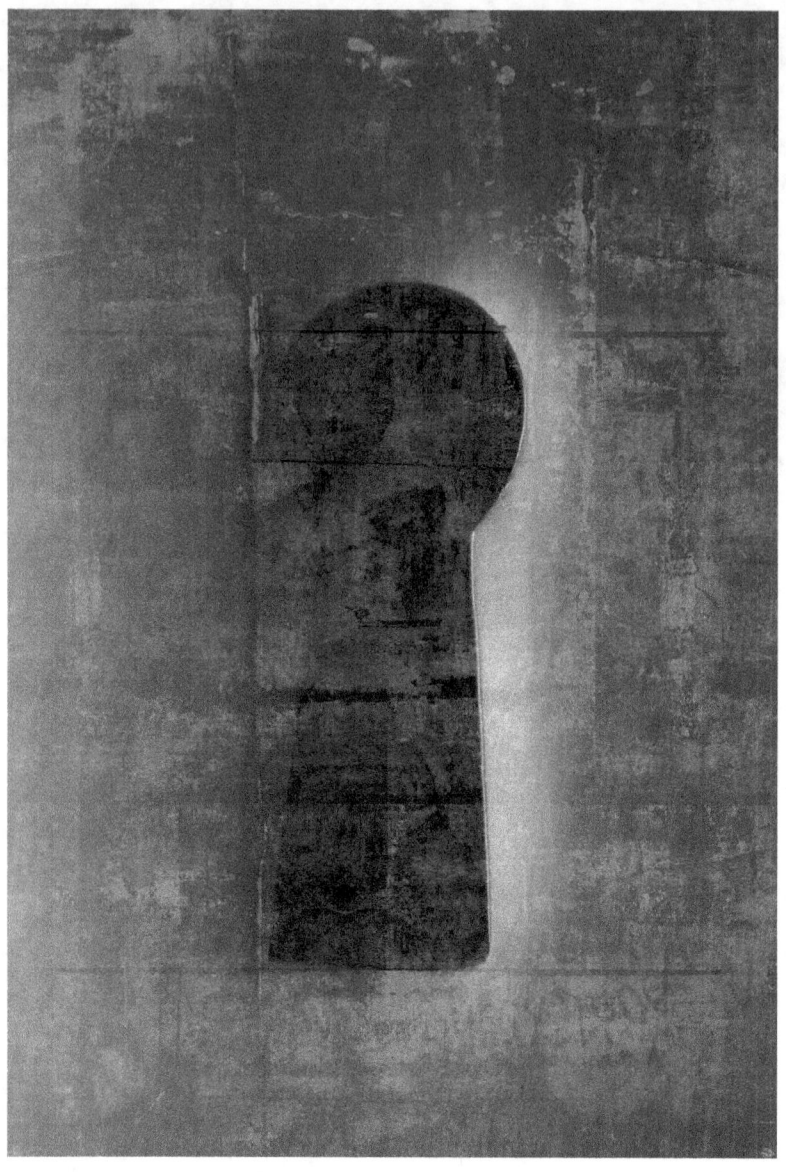

For about five years I went to therapy along with the abusive foster mother I lived with. She'd spend 30 minutes complaining about me. That didn't help me at all.

But recently I started thinking I needed therapy—with a good therapist—and I found a counselor through my school. But to understand how therapy is supposed to work, and how to trust a therapist, I spoke to Elizabeth Kandall, a psychologist who started the Children's Psychotherapy Project in New York City (now known as A Home Within).

Elizabeth is a short, brunette woman. She was dressed in dark clothes and had a tranquil, patient air about her. Like many other therapists, she refused to give me any definite answers. I felt she wanted me to figure out things by myself, which was cool.

When I asked her to explain the connection between anger and abuse, she acted just like you'd expect a therapist to act, asking me, "What do you think it is?"

> **Part of our brain remembers how we felt in the past, even when our conscious mind has forgotten it.**

I surprised myself by telling the truth clearly. I said, "I think anger's a symptom of abuse. Severe anger—it's uncontrollable. It doesn't help you, it hurts you, it messes you up."

"So you see it as uncontrollable, unfocused, self-destructive anger?" she said.

I was like, "All right. I know that. So what can I do about it?"

Elizabeth said it might be helpful to think about the unconscious. That's the idea that part of our brain remembers how we felt in the past, even when our conscious mind has forgotten it.

Past feelings—like helplessness or fear—that we have in our unconscious minds can affect how we feel in the present. For example, even if you're out of a dangerous situation, like an abusive home, your unconscious might still believe you're in danger.

"It's like the unconscious isn't sure that the past is all over," Elizabeth explained. "Logically, in your wakeful mind, you can say it's really over—like you could say, 'I'm not 3 years old anymore.' But in your unconscious mind it's still present."

I knew what she meant. My mother scolding me reminds me of my former foster mother's abuse, and the humiliation my biological mother put me through. My sister restricting me reminds me of restrictions my former foster mother placed on me, like making me use separate plates and spoons from her biological family.

Of course, I wanted to know how to convince your unconscious that the danger is over. Elizabeth said you have to explore what your past means to you, how your past relates to the present, and what makes you still feel in danger. That might help your fear go away.

Elizabeth said therapy should be a relationship where you can reflect on your past experiences and see how those experiences might still be affecting you today. (The therapist can help you see connections or patterns that you might not be able to.) "It's a chance to take stock and think about what's going on, instead of just continuing to repeat it," she said.

Still, it's not easy for those of us whose trust has been betrayed to trust a therapist with our stories. Some of us don't open up at all; others open up too quickly. "People respond to feelings of being unsafe sometimes by running headlong into danger. That sets up another dangerous situation," she told me.

Elizabeth said we should bring along all our skepticism and distrust when we meet a therapist. "Stay as tight as you need to for as long as you need to," she said, but also ask yourself if you might benefit by opening up. Then take slow, progressive steps to see if the therapist can earn your trust.

If you're thinking, "Uh-oh, I don't trust this person," you might want to ask yourself, "Is it me? Do I go 'Uh-oh,' to everybody? Or is it something about this person?"

You might also talk to the therapist about all of the things you're afraid of, and explain what you need. You can see why you need the things you do, and you can judge whether someone really is trying to understand you.

HOW TO CHILL OUT

An interview with Toni Heineman, a therapist and director of A Home Within in San Francisco, California

Q How do you recognize that you have a problem with anger?

A: Figure out whether the intensity of your feeling matches the situation that's making you mad. If someone is a little bit mean to you, and you want to kill them, that's a problem. Or if someone is extremely mean to you, and you only feel a little bit mad, that's also a problem. Your anger should match the situation.

The second step is identifying what you're really upset about. If you're driving and someone cuts you off, and you want to ram your car into the other car, you're probably upset about something else. You need to figure out what that is.

Q How does someone develop an anger problem?

A: Often the problem is that, early on, a child doesn't learn that there can be different levels of anger. If the people around that child were brutally angry over something very small or nothing at all, like a mother beating a child over a few dollars, then a child learns that if there's something to be angry about, the only option is to be furious. The child also learns that he can't be angry at all in return, or that the anger has to be put on someone else, like a stranger.

Q So what can you do when you get mad?

A: You want to figure out some ways to help yourself calm down before you decide to take any action. One way to stay calm is to ask yourself, "If I take this action (like punching someone), will it get me what I want?" You want to try to act in your own best interest. If you're mouthing off to a cop, you might want to say, "Wait a minute, he has a baton and a gun. Maybe screaming at him is not in my best interest."

Q What are some ways to calm down?

A: The best thing to do is to get out of a situation, either physically or in your head. If you're in an argument, you can try to say, "I'm feeling really angry. Can we talk later when I feel calmer?" You can leave, go for a walk and swear to yourself if you want, or go for a run and feel a little better.

You can also try putting things into words. Sometimes in therapy, my clients will come late to an appointment on purpose. That's one way of expressing anger. A better way might be to come in and say, "I was thinking of coming late because I'm so mad at you." Then we can talk about why you're mad.

I don't care how mad you are, you can't hit. Just like there's no excuse for domestic violence, there's no excuse for hitting someone else.

Q How can therapy or anger management help?

A: Often in your life, something goes wrong and you don't even know why. In therapy, you can figure out that it's a pattern. Even after you realize you get too angry too often, it's hard to change. Eventually, though, you think, "I need to change something, because if I don't, I'm going to keep doing it again, and it's hurting me to keep doing this." After that, instead of just acting on how you feel, you can recognize what's going on and change the way you react.

It takes a lot of work, because you're learning those coping skills late.

When you're little, you learn certain habits. Now you have to unlearn the bad ones and learn new ones. You have to say, "I have a problem, and there's nothing I can do to change that my mother beat me and she shouldn't have, or that someone hurt me and it was unfair. I can change the way I treat people, and I can try to put myself in situations with people who will treat me well."

Q What about when you can't react to anger in a healthy way, like your staff won't let you go out and take a walk or you can't avoid someone who's mean?

A: No one should have to bear the burden of someone else losing control. But in an impossible situation, the only way to reasonably deal with that is to try to remain calm and just let it go. If you let other people's unfair actions upset you, it'll make you crazy. If you're powerless, the only way to have power is to tune out, to daydream, to remove yourself from the situation in your own mind. Once they put you in an incredibly helpless situation and you lose control, they have the power.

ABOUT YOUTH COMMUNICATION

Youth Communication, founded in 1980, is a nonprofit educational publishing company located in New York City. Its mission is to help marginalized teens develop their full potential through reading and writing, so that they can succeed in school and at work and contribute to their communities.

Youth Communication publishes true stories by teens that are developed in a rigorous writing program. It offers more than 50 books that adults can use to engage reluctant teen readers on an array of topics including peer pressure, school, sex, and relationships. The stories also appear in two award-winning magazines, *YCteen* and *Represent,* and on the website (www.youthcomm.org), and are frequently reprinted in popular and professional magazines and textbooks. Youth Communication offers hundreds of lessons, complete leader's guides, and professional development to guide educators in using the stories to help teens improve their academic, social, and emotional skills.

Youth Communication's stories, written by a diverse group of teen writers, are uniquely compelling to peers who do not see their experiences reflected in mainstream reading materials. They motivate teens to read and write, encourage good values, and show teens how to make positive changes in their lives.

You can access many of the stories and sample lessons for free at www.youthcomm.org. For more information on Youth Communication's products and services, contact Loretta Chan at 212-279-0708, x115, or lchan@youthcomm.org.

Youth Communication
224 West 29th Street, 2nd Floor
New York, NY 10001
212-279-0708
www.youthcomm.org

ABOUT THE EDITOR

Laura Longhine is the editorial director at Youth Communication, where she oversees editorial work on the organization's books, websites, and magazines. She edited *Represent,* Youth Communication's magazine by and for teens in foster care, for three years.

Prior to joining Youth Communication, Laura was a staff writer at the *Free Times,* an alt-weekly in South Carolina, and a freelance reporter for various publications. Her stories have been published in *The New York Times, Legal Affairs,* newyorkmetro.com, and *Child Welfare Watch.* She has a bachelor's in English from Tufts University and a master's in journalism from Columbia University.

Laura is also the editor of several other books by Youth Communication, including *Real Men: Urban Teens Write About How to Be a Man* and *Analyze This! A Teen Guide to Therapy and Getting Help.*

Real Teen Voices Series

Pressure

True Stories by Teens About Stress
edited by Al Desetta of Youth Communication

Stress hits these teen writers from all angles; they're feeling the pressure at school, at home, and in their relationships. The young writers describe their stress-relief techniques, including exercise, music, writing, and more. The collection includes tips for cooling down and inspiring examples of perseverance. For ages 13 & up.

Rage

True Stories by Teens About Anger
edited by Laura Longhine of Youth Communication

The teen writers in *Rage* have plenty of reasons to be angry: parental abuse, street violence, peer pressure, feeling powerless, and more. The writers give honest advice and talk about their anger management skills as they struggle to gain control of their emotions and stop hurting others—and themselves. For ages 13 & up.

Vicious

True Stories by Teens About Bullying
edited by Hope Vanderberg of Youth Communication

Essays by teens address bullying: physical, verbal, relational, and cyber. These stories will appeal to readers because the cruelty and hurt are unmistakably real—and the reactions of the writers are sometimes cringe-worthy, often admirable, and always believable. For ages 13 & up.

Interested in purchasing multiple quantities and receiving volume discounts?
Contact edsales@freespirit.com or call 1.800.735.7323 and ask for Education Sales.

Many Free Spirit authors are available for speaking engagements, workshops, and keynotes. Contact speakers@freespirit.com or call 1.800.735.7323.

For pricing information, to place an order, or to request a free catalog, contact:

**Free Spirit Publishing Inc.
217 Fifth Avenue North • Suite 200 • Minneapolis, MN 55401-1299
toll-free 800.735.7323 • local 612.338.2068 • fax 612.337.5050**
help4kids@freespirit.com • www.freespirit.com

BACK COVER MATERIAL

RAGE

True Stories by Teens About Anger

Tormented by her painful past, Natasha feels anger eating at her like cancer until she learns to let it out.

Joseph was physically and sexually abused—but some of his rage subsides when he finds a foster mom who respects him.

Dealing with a troubled childhood, Shateek learns to channel his anger into success on the wrestling mat.

The writers in *Rage* have plenty of reasons to be angry: parental abuse, street violence, peer pressure, and more. Their stories are grippingly honest. They also offer realistic advice and anger management skills these teens have used in their struggle to gain control of their emotions and stop hurting others—and themselves. The resilience they find within themselves is inspiring.

Index

A

Abandonment,
  families working together after, *90, 92*
  by fathers, *89, 90, 92, 94, 96, 98*
Abuse,
  anger as symptom of, *4, 5, 7, 19, 210*
  defining, *194, 195*
  fighting as response to, *178*
  neglect, *46, 47*
  physical, *5, 8, 19, 118, 175, 194*
  repeating cycle of, *182, 197, 198, 199, 201*
  retaining in unconscious mind, *211*
  self-mutilation, *75, 82, 178*
  sexual, *19, 118, 141, 146*
  verbal, *5, 50, 75, 164, 165, 167, 175*
  witnessing, between parents, *17, 19*
Alcoholism in families, *92, 118, 202*
Anger,
  accepting responsibility for, *204*
  from being bullied, *33, 79, 176*
  dangers from holding in, *56*
  dangers of ignoring, *71*
  developing problem with, *217*
  drugs and, *28*
  emotions related to, *24*
  fear of expressing, *44, 46, 51, 179*

internal effects of, *99*
positive aspects of, *11, 100*
recognizing having problem with, *7, 217*
recognizing real cause of, *217*
as symptom of abuse, *4, 5, 7, 19, 210*

Anger management therapy, *21, 23, 24, 25, 219*

Anxiety, characteristics and causes of high, *201*

Anxiety, Phobias, & Panic (Peurifoy), *201, 202, 206*

Appearance, being bullied because of, *33*

B

Bullying,
appearance and race as reason for being target of, *33*
as response to violence, *176*
sexual orientation as reason for being target of, *141, 142*
violent response to, *79, 142, 144*

Butcher, Marc Anthony, *98, 99*

C

Change,
attempting to, *60, 62, 63, 64, 65, 144*
difficulties of, *67, 68, 70, 71, 183, 219*
motivation for, *182*

Cleaning, as control strategy, *14*

Control,
excessive need to be in, *202, 204*
inability to handle emotions, *5*
relying on others for, *72*

Control strategies,

analyzing situation, *218*
avoiding anger-producing situations, *204*
breathing techniques, *25, 206*
cleaning, *14*
counting, *25*
knitting, *27*
meditation, *36*
playing sports, *105, 107, 108, 110, 111, 112, 114, 168*
pleasant imagery, *25*
prayer, *11*
removing self from situation, *85, 218, 219*
sports, *105, 107, 108, 110, 111, 112, 114, 168*
walking, *7, 8*
writing,
  journaling, *131, 134, 135, 151, 152, 204*
  poetry, *25, 137, 154, 155, 161*
  stories, *25, 152*
  thought process sheets, *125*
See also Therapy, Coping skills,
See Control strategies,
Creative writing, as control strategy, *25, 152*
Crippled Enigma, *155, 157, 158, 160*
Cutting self, *75*

D

Detention centers, *80*
Dreams, as wake-up calls, *158, 160*
Drugs and anger, *28*

E

Ego, *67*
Emotions,
  accepting responsibility for, *204*
  dangers of holding in, *56*
  dangers of ignoring, *71*

hiding, *51*
inability to control, *5, 67, 68*
related to anger, *24*
roller coaster nature of, *52, 54*
in unconscious mind, *211*
Emotions, expressing,
by acts of rage, *120, 121*
communicating face-to-face, *161*
family taboos against, *21, 23*
fear of, *44, 46, 51, 179*
importance of learning, *178, 179*
pain relief from, *85, 122, 124*
relief derived from, *24, 25*
by self-mutilation, *75, 82, 178*
by writing, journaling, *131, 134, 135, 151, 152, 204*
poetry, *25, 137, 154, 155, 161*
stories, *25, 152*
thought process sheets, *125*
Excelsior Youth Center, *121, 122, 124, 125, 127*

F

Families,
alcoholism in, *92, 202*
in chaos, *46, 47*
death in, *105, 110, 131, 135, 151*
growing up in abusive,
neglect, *46, 47*
physical, *5, 19, 175, 194*
seeing violence between parents, *17, 19*
sexual, *19, 141, 146*
stays in unconscious mind, *211*

telling others about, *186*
verbal, *5, 75, 175*
repeating cycle of abuse, *182, 197, 198, 199, 201*
with rigid attitudes, *202*
supportive, *11, 12*
taboos against expressing feelings, *21, 23*
working together after abandonment by father, *90, 92*
Fathers,
　abandonment by, *89, 90, 92, 94, 96, 98*
　seeing violence between mothers and, *17, 19*
Fear and rage, *19, 20*
Feelings,
　See Emotions; Emotions, expressing,
Fighting,
　attempting to avoid, *60, 62, 63, 64, 65*
　as response to abuse, *178*
　as response to bullying, *79, 142, 144*
Foster homes,
　abuse in, *168, 169*
　　being bullied, *141, 142*
　　physical, *5, 8, 118*
　　sexual, *118*
　　treatment as second-class, *48, 50*
　　verbal, *5, 50, 164, 165, 167*
　experiencing good, *169, 171*
　feeling alone in, *134*
　loving, *10, 11*
　moving among, *118*
Friends, *124*

G

Girls' Group, *83, 85, 86*
Goals, achieving, *114*

Graham Windham treatment center, *80, 82, 83, 85, 86*

Group homes,
difficulties living in, *142, 179, 180*
as halfway houses, *127*
residential treatment centers, *21, 23, 24, 25, 27, 80, 82, 83, 85, 86, 121, 122, 124, 125, 127*
rumors about, *167*

Gspoetry, *155, 157*

H

Halfway houses, *127*

Hate, effect on self, *99*

Homosexuality,
acceptance of, *144, 145*
being bullied because of, *141, 142*
hiding, *142*

J

Journaling, as control strategy, *131, 134, 135, 151, 152, 204*

Juvenile justice system,
courts, *78, 79, 80*
facilities after being arrested, *21*
residential treatment centers, *80, 82, 83, 85, 86*

K

Kandall, Elizabeth, *210*

Karate, as control strategy, *33, 34, 36, 37, 39, 40*

Knitting, as control strategy, *27*

L

Love,
fearing being hurt by, *7*
in foster homes, *10, 11*

sense of security from, *52*

M

Marijuana and anger, *28*

Meditation, as control strategy, *36*

N

Neglect, as form of abuse, *46, 47*

P

Panic attacks, *54, 55, 56*

Parents, seeing violence between, *17, 19*

Past, alive in unconscious mind, *211*

Personas, danger of false, *155, 157, 158, 160, 161*

Peurifoy, Reneau Z., *201, 202, 206*

Physical abuse, *5, 8, 19, 118, 175, 194*

Pleasant imagery, using, *25*

Poetry writing, as control strategy, *25, 137, 154, 155, 161*

Positive Messages: For Young Men Growing Up Without Their Fathers (Butcher), *98*

Prayer, as control strategy, *11*

Pride, *67*

R

Race, being bullied because of, *33*

Represent (magazine), *138*

Residential treatment centers (RTCs), *21, 23, 24, 25, 27, 80, 82, 83, 85, 86, 121, 122, 124, 125, 127*

Role models,
 becoming one, *40*
 having, *36, 37*

Running away, *8, 10*

S

Security, love gives sense of, *52*

Self-confidence,
 development of, *37*
 lack of, *50*
Self-discipline,
 development of, *37*
Self-esteem,
 self-mutilation and, *75, 82*
 verbal abuse, *75*
Self-mutilation, *75, 82, 178*
Self-respect, learning, *82*
Sexual abuse, *19, 118, 141, 146*
Sexual orientation,
 acceptance of, *144, 145*
 being bullied because of, *141, 142*
 hiding, *142*
Sports,
 ability in, and acceptance by others, *95*
 channeling anger through, *105, 107, 108, 110, 111, 112, 114, 168*
 learning by self, *94*
Stories, writing to express emotions, *25, 152*
Suicide,
 attempted, *180*
 thoughts of, *176, 178, 179*

T

Therapy,
 anger management, *21, 23, 24, 25, 219*
 characteristics of effective, *187, 189, 190*
 opening up at right pace, *213*
 recognizing need for, *198, 199*
 relationship described, *213*
 at residential centers, *21, 23, 24, 25, 27, 83, 85, 86, 121, 122, 124, 125, 127*
 trust is essential, *186, 187, 189, 213*

Thought process sheets, *125*
Time-outs, *122, 124*
Trust, as essential part of therapy, *186, 187, 189, 213*

U
Unconscious mind, *211*

V
Verbal abuse, *5, 50, 75, 164, 165, 167, 175*

W
Walking, as control strategy, *7, 8*
Weed and anger, *28*
Worthlessness, feelings of, *50*
Wrestling, as control strategy, *105, 107, 108, 110, 111, 112, 114*
Writing, as control strategy,
   journaling, *131, 134, 135, 151, 152, 204*
   poetry, *25, 137, 154, 155, 161*

stories, *25, 152*
thought process sheets, *125*

www.ingramcontent.com/pod-product-compliance
Lightning Source LLC
Chambersburg PA
CBHW060600230426
43670CB00011B/1903